Social Media Explained
Untangling the World's Most Misunderstood Business Trend

By Mark W. Schaefer

This publication is designed to provide accurate and authoritative information in regard to the subject matter covered. it is sold with the understanding that neither the author nor the pub-lisher is engaged in rendering legal, accounting, or other professional service. If legal advice or other expert assistance is required, the services of a competent professional person should be sought.
    - From a Declaration of Principles jointly adopted by a Committee of the American Bar Association and a Committee of Publishers.

Schaefer Marketing Solutions
www.businessesGROW.com

First Edition: January 2014

Publisher is not responsible for websites (or their content) that are not owned by the publisher.

Interior Layout and Design by Strawesome Illustration & Design

Library of Congress Cataloging-in-Publication Data

Schaefer, Mark W.
Social Media Explained: Untangling the World's Most
Misunderstood Business Trend

Mark W. Schaefer - 1st ed.

ISBN
978-0-615-84003-1

Contents

Section One

The Five Most Important Things You Need to Know about Social Media Marketing

Section Two

The Five Most Difficult Questions You'll Face

Section Three

A Social Media Primer   123

Blogs
Podcasting
Twitter
Facebook
LinkedIn
Pinterest
Google+
YouTube
SlideShare
Photo sites

May I have your attention please?

If you're a busy executive doing the job that used to be three jobs, balancing a hectic travel schedule with family time, and struggling to keep up with the latest business trends, I want you to know that I have been in your shoes, and I feel your pain.

And now on top of everything, they want a social media strategy out of you!

By now you've heard enough about the potential of marketing through social media platforms like Facebook, YouTube and Twitter to know this is a significant, unstoppable force. For many in today's world, the social web is the preferred method of connecting, communicating, learning, and discovering products and service. It's the place where consumers go online to discuss their purchases, seek advice, offer reviews, and complain. Increasing amounts of the marketing budget are being thrown into this mystifying world.

Yet study after study confirms "executive confusion" over what to do about the social media trend and how to harness its power. Even most CMOs who are immersed in this world are unclear on the strategy, the benefits, and the purpose of social media in the context of a broader marketing effort.

The world is expecting your company or department to "be social," with a blog, Facebook page, and the rest of the social media tsunami. At the same time, it's often difficult to see where and how to influence these online conversations, let alone measure their impact. You may be finding it difficult to devote significant resources—financial or human—to an activity whose precise impact on the bottom line remains unclear.

In fact, you might find yourself struggling to even know what questions to ask. You don't have time to loll around on Twitter and Facebook all day to find out. Trying to keep up feels like taking a drink from a fire hydrant, doesn't it? If you're not engaged, you're probably worried that you're falling behind fast.

I wrote this book for you – the overwhelmed sales and marketing professional, business owner, or CMO who needs to understand enough about what is going on in this space to make some decisions. This book explains how social media marketing works, in plain English.

After reading this book, you will not be a social media expert, but you probably don't need to be. To be an effective leader, you simply have to know enough to **ask the right questions**. And you will.

Social Media Explained is divided into four short sections. The first section covers the foundational concepts of how social media works across any organization, and across any social media platform. If you understand these five important concepts, you will understand the basics of social media marketing, no matter where it takes us in the future.

Section two covers the five most common questions you're probably getting from your boss and gives you enough ammo to answer them.

The third part is a case study that illustrates how these concepts work in action.

Finally, I'll give you a clear-eyed view of some of the major social media platforms so you can be conversant about them.

This is all very practical, no-nonsense stuff that will help you navigate the new world of social media marketing even if you have never seen a tweet!

Now, I promise that I'm going to help you figure this stuff out, but you have to pay attention. I need you to be here now. Put down the phone. Turn off the laptop. Answer the text messages later. See ... I know you, don't I?

If you really pay attention to this book – maybe even make a few notes along the way – you'll know enough to ask the right questions, the questions that are going to save you a lot of time, money, and heartache down the road.

In order to get the most out of this book, I need your un-divided attention for 90 minutes. Even if you don't like books, you can handle this one. It's short and I'll do my part to keep you interested. Plus, it has cartoons from my friend Joey Strawn! What more can you ask for?

Are you with me? REALLY with me?

All right. Let's get to work.

Section One

The five foundational social media strategies

Chapter One

Humans buy from humans

We're going to start our big discussion of social media by going hundreds of years into the past to the first medieval marketplaces of Europe. Trust me. This is leading somewhere.

As far as scholars can tell, formal marketplaces were first created in Europe around the year 1,000 AD. They solved a problem. Villages were competing with other villages for commerce. Unlicensed hucksters went from town to town and the whole thing was rather inefficient until a few rules were applied to the mess, usually by the local church leaders.

Here were some of the characteristics of these newly-organized markets:

It was highly personal and interactive. You stood face to face with your seller, looked them in the eye, and bought with a firm handshake. You purchased goods from people you knew and trusted. You may have even passed their farm or workshop on the way to the market. And people expected transparency – you could see the goods you were buying right before you.

There was immediacy. If somebody felt wronged or cheated, you knew it right away because they were going to be knocking on your door. Feedback on quality, service, and pricing was constant and immediate.

Success depended on word of mouth recommendations. There was no advertising, mass media, or PR spin back then. If you wronged a buyer, word would spread throughout your market-place like a plague (well, perhaps that's a poor analogy!). So you needed to treat people right ... and maybe even do a little extra for your power buyers.

There was a primal need to connect. It wasn't just about buying and selling. There was a social aspect to these marketplaces and that was part of the fun. People inherently like to talk about the news, the local gossip, and themselves.

So the first marketplaces were social-based, intimate places to do business and that's the way it was for centuries.

Then around 1439 everything changed.

The printing press was invented and flyers, newspapers and magazines soon followed. This ushered in an era of advertising, which was significant because we took our first step away from the person-to-person interactions that were the very foundation for selling and buying for centuries.

Still, most commerce was conducted with neighbors and the small family-owned businesses on every street corner. But that changed forever on November 2, 1920 when KDKA, the first commercial broadcast radio station went on the air in Pittsburgh, PA. The era of mass communications had begun.

We could not have known it at the time, but we had just bought ourselves a one-way ticket as far from our customers as we could get. In fact, we created a permanent digital divide between us.

There was nothing personal about it. We bought massive amounts of airtime, produced our slick ads and waited for something to happen. Television, the Internet, and websites created even more opportunities to reach massive numbers of customers quickly and cost-effectively.

Maybe this is where you are with your company today. Taking out ads. Sending out press releases. Posting deals on your website.

The problem is, many of these traditional ways we communicated and marketed to our customers are evaporating.

- The Newspaper Association of America reports that, adjusted for inflation, newspaper advertising revenue is down to 1950s levels. Nearly every major newspaper is losing their print circulation and many cities are without a printed daily newspaper at all. We are seeing the same trend in other parts of the world, too.

- Nielsen reports that the number of hours of television viewed by Americans is in decline for the first time in the history of television. There is no such thing as "regularly scheduled programming" any longer. People are more likely to be watching their favorite programs via Hulu or Netflix, or buying a series for their iPad, skipping right through the commercials.

- Even websites are under attack. Between 2010-2012, two-thirds of the Fortune 500 companies had fewer visitors to their websites.

The beginning of the social media era

If the traditional media channels are fading away, where are all these people going? You probably know by now. The social web. Social media platforms like Facebook, Twitter, and Pinterest are becoming the new town squares to exchange news, photos, videos, and our personal life events. They are also becoming the preferred place to go to find products and answers to problems.

Edison Research found that 80 percent of Americans under the age of 24 had a Facebook account and half of them accessed it at least once a day. This may be the most significant immersion in a brand we have ever witnessed. Facebook is by far the largest media entity in history.

Now this is where it gets interesting, because we're going back to the future! Let's look at the characteristics of the social web:

It is highly personal and interactive. To succeed on the social web, you have to forget about being B2B or B2C. You have to have a strategy to be P2P – person to person. Social media is SO-CIAL. People are sick of being sold to, advertised to, and marketed to. They don't go on Facebook to see your new line of ball bearings. They are going there to play Farmville and see stupid pictures of cats. But they WILL spend time with individuals who are there to help them make money, save money, save time, be happier, or make them smile.

There is immediacy. If somebody is mad at you or your company, you are going to hear about it. People are probably out on the web right now talking about you and it may not all be good. If you're not immersed in the web you are going to miss all this action. You have to be prepared to LISTEN to what's going on out there and respond, just like in the days of the medieval market.

Success depends on word of mouth recommendations. We are in an era where EVERYBODY can publish. Anybody with In-ternet access and a keyboard can write reviews, create blog posts, and record videos for the world to see. Influence has been democratized. If you operate a reputable company, this is a good thing. Word of your good deeds will spread across the world. The social web also allows an unprecedented opportunity to discover, and nurture powerful brand advocates you may not have even known about before.

There is a primal need to connect. Nobody MUST spend time on the social web. People want to be there because this is the new town square ... except that instead of sharing an opinion to their six neighbors, it might be going out to 6,000 Twitter followers.

Back to the future

The fact of the matter is that these values and expectations have been shared between buyers and sellers for centuries. We simply interrupted the natural course of business for about 100 years with the introduction of mass media. We learned that we can sell very efficiently by broadcasting ads through radio, TV and the Internet — and we still can — but we also created a permanent digital divide between ourselves and our customers. The human side of business that people crave was disengaged when we turned exclusively to mass advertising.

Like many executives, you may be freaking out about exposing your company to other human beings on Facebook or other social channels. We're conditioned to broadcast and advertise, not to allow our customers talk back. One executive lamented to me, "Can't we make this go away? It looks like the deer have guns!" No, we can't make this go away. Ignoring this trend is like ignoring the existence of newspapers or televisions. That seems kind of silly, right?

But another way to look at this is that the social web is simply bringing us back to our marketplace roots where personal connection, immediacy, and word of mouth validation are the most important marketing considerations.

We're returning to the way people have ALWAYS wanted to buy from us – person to person. Humans buy from humans. And now you have the opportunity to humanize your company and join in the commercial renaissance, too.

One of my favorite case studies to illustrate the power of

community is a family-owned bakery in Houston called Dessert Gallery. The business has a small but loyal Facebook following of less than 3,000 fans. However, a study by Rice University found that this audience was providing profound benefits to the bakery including:

- 36 percent more visits than non-Facebook customers

- 45 percent more of their dining budget spent at the bakery

- 33 percent spent more at the bakery than at other restaurants

- Greater emotional attachment to the brand

The owner successfully uses her Facebook page to gain marketing insight, address customer problems, communicate promotions, and get feedback on new product ideas.

But what I like most about this example is an interview I saw with the owner. She commented that as she runs her business, she would not normally have too much time for customer interaction. But through social media, she can connect with hundreds of people each week in a personal and human way. She can offer them insights, comments, and opportunities to engage through contests and polls. And she loves to reward and delight people on her Facebook page with free cookies and brownies!

I use this case study in my classes and ask the question ... "Is this sustainable? Can the owner continue to grow her business through social media connections?"

The answer always comes back, "Yes, if you are truly building loyalty in the process." And as you will see in the next chapter, that is EXACTLY the opportunity before us.

Questions leaders need to consider

1. If my company provided a human face to our customers through our content, what would that look like?

2. In what ways can we become more human and accessible to our customers? How does our company culture help or hurt that process?

3. Who should be the face of our company? Are there many employees already representing our company today on the social web -- whether we know it or not? How can we get them to help us?

Chapter Two

The theory of small interactions

The other day I saw this remarkable photo on the Internet. A guy had tattooed a Nike "swoosh" symbol on the side of his foot.

It made me pause and think. Isn't that amazing? Isn't that what we all want our companies to achieve – to have people love us so much they permanently decorate their bodies with our company logo?

And I began to wonder, how do we get customers to that point? That guy didn't try on his first pair of sneakers and run to the tattoo parlor. This bold and permanent symbol was the result of years of consistent, small interactions with the brand that left him so engaged and delighted that he committed the ultimate act of customer loyalty.

These small interactions are what bring us together as people, and it's what brings us together as loyal customers. To demonstrate, I want to take you back a few years – not 1,000 years this time – but just far enough back that you can remember when you were invited to your first birthday party.

Think for a moment about your very first day of school. You were nervous, probably a little scared, and maybe even overwhelmed by this big, noisy room. There was this strange colorful classroom and lots of people you didn't know all proudly wearing their new school clothes. It may have been your first meeting with an adult role model who wasn't a relative.

And then something wonderful happened. You found somebody to talk to. Maybe they admired your Disney lunch box or your bright white tennis shoes. But you got their attention. You had made your first school friend. Next thing you know, you're playing together on the playground, helping each other with homework, maybe even going to their home after school to play. Perhaps you started to go to sleep-overs. You were beginning to trust each other, to rely on each other, and form a close bond.

Finally, after weeks or months, that magical event happened. You get invited to the birthday party! What a great feeling! Do you remember it? All those small interactions paid off -- over homework, on the playground, and in the lunch room. You became part of an inner circle.

It's not just a brand. It's a Buddy.

We form our deepest relationships with companies the same way. Our favorite products are not just brands – over time they become our friends and this is a key idea behind social media's role in the marketing mix. Here's an example of what I mean. I've been going to Home Depot for 20 years and have spent untold thousands of dollars on home improvement and landscaping materials. Although I have not tattooed their logo on any part of my body, I am a totally loyal customer.

A few months ago, I bought a dozen small bushes for my front yard. About half of them died. The store has a one-year guarantee on its plants so I took a picture of the dead plants (instead of uprooting them and carrying the six dirt balls in my car) and, with receipt in hand, went to the store for a refund.

When I presented my claim to the service clerk I was told that I would have to drive home, dig up the plants, and show the actual evidence before I could get my refund. When I explained that I wasn't about to make another 40-minute round-trip visit to get the dead plants, the clerk said, "Well, for all we know that could be a picture of your neighbor's yard."

I had a very sudden and unexpected feeling of personal betrayal. You see, Home Depot was not just a brand. It was a buddy. I felt like my friend was calling me a liar. After all we have been through? The epic kitchen remodeling? The new tile in the bathroom? The rock garden? After all that, my friend wasn't about to help me out on $20 worth of plants?

I caught myself actually feeling jilted ... and then feeling a little silly about it. For decades, I had been loyal to Home Depot ... but I wasn't feeling the love back. Why would I expect anything in return? They were just a big, faceless company, right?

And yet, don't we form these strong relationships with our favorite brands just like we form a friendship? Friendships don't happen immediately. It takes a history of small interactions that slowly builds trust, and eventually an emotional bond.

Through this experience with Home Depot, I didn't feel any P2P love. I felt it was B2N — Business to Nobody.

Let's rewind the clock and see how this could have been much different. What could Home Depot have done to provide a constant drip, drip, drip of consistent, helpful, small interactions (or "provocations") that would have built our "friendship?"

A few years ago, I signed up for the Home Depot Garden Club. Since I buy so much stuff from them, I figured I would get some good deals for my loyalty. Turns out it was a huge bust. All I got were some flyers and useless emails. Let's create a plan where a series of small, helpful interactions would lead to loyalty and increased purchases:

- Home Depot has a record of everything I have ever purchased. Why wouldn't they send me automated offers based on what I have bought, the season of the year, and the region where I live? They could actually forecast my needs.

- Even better, wouldn't it be cool if I received a tweet reminding me to give my bushes a little extra water because of the drought conditions in my area? Or maybe offer me a free drought-resistant plant that they just introduced?

- These small interactions could lead me to helpful tips on the Home Depot site. They have nearly 11,000 posts and YouTube videos about gardening ideas and yet I probably would not think to go there unless they make an effort to connect with me in a way that would lead me to their blog.

- Once I arrive at their site, I would like to log-in to a personal area where I can see an inventory of every plant I have bought and reminders of fertilizer and pruning needs. Why not have a "buy now" button and have my purchase delivered to me the next day or waiting for pick-up at the store?

- I would like to be invited to submit photos of my landscaping accomplishments to Instagram or their Facebook page. After all that sweaty work, why not show off the results and become inspired by the work of others?

- Finally, when my bushes die, it would be nice for the customer service agent to ask me if I am a member of the Garden Club, look at my purchase history, confirm that I bought the plants and be empowered to solve my problem on the spot.

You can see how these small, consistent, meaningful interactions would absolutely lead to customer loyalty, word of mouth recommendations, and increased purchases.

Now notice that in my list of ideas I never mentioned coupons. Fact is, loyal customers connect with their favorite brands on the web out of love, not just for deals. A study from Edison Research showed that 57 percent of American social media users follow a brand on Facebook for no other reason than they have an affinity for the company.

And that affinity can create powerful results. The study also shows that one-third of social media users purchase more from a brand after they begin to follow them on a social media account.

Marketing's primary goal is to reach consumers at those moments that influence purchasing behavior. Social media seems perfect for that role: it's the only form of marketing that can touch consumers at each and every stage in the buying process, from when they're comparing products right through the period after a purchase. And, their experience with a brand and potential advocacy influences others. Increasingly, social media content is also being used to reward and nurture established customers.

By now you are probably starting to get a sense of how things work on the social web so I want to push your thinking a little further.

The powerful interactions I've described are two-way and mutually-beneficial. In school, I helped my friend with his homework and he helped me. I went to his house to play and he came to mine. I went to his birthday party and he came to mine. That two-way connection is also how we build our best business connections.

So why do we think about relationships in the online world so differently? Why is all of our effort placed on dragging people to OUR website? To comment on OUR blog? To like OUR Facebook page?

The one thing missing in almost any social media strategy I see is a plan for company representatives to actually go spend some time at the customer's "house."

Why is the metric for success always the number of comments or likes you have on your page, rather than the number of likes and comments your company gives away on other pages? Shouldn't the effort be at least equal?

This default position of driving people to your page is easy because it is so much simpler measuring your "likes" and comments as a metric of success. It's the popular thing to do, but I'd like you to start questioning if it is the RIGHT thing to do for a long-term strategy aimed at building loyal relationships.

As we will see in Section 2, social media can deliver a lot to a company – brand awareness, market intelligence, customer insight, and a cost-effective platform for customer service, to name a few.

But from a business perspective, this is the ideal place for social media in the sales funnel – creating these small, consistent interactions that delight, educate, and inspire people to become customers and then reward their loyalty with personalized attention and meaningful content.

A company doing it right

Although McDonalds is a multinational megabrand, it still realizes the importance of small, consistent personal interactions.

If you follow the brand on Twitter or Facebook, most posts are followed by an employee's initials. You know WHO is sending you that message. In addition to the main @McDonalds handle on Twitter, each person speaking in social media for the brand has a personal page where they are empowered to get into deeper conversations with customers about McDonalds. A link on the page connects you with the photos and profiles of everybody who is tweeting and posting for the company. In fact, many interactions are followed up with a hand-written note sent via "snail mail" to take social interactions not only offline, but back to the restaurants. These interactions are authentic and human. A few fans have even created friendships with their favorite McDonalds Tweeters!

Likewise, the company's PR department has "adopted" important bloggers in their industry. The PR professionals spend time going to the blogger's "house" to learn about the issues that are important to them. The McDonalds employees may comment on the blogs, help promote them and send them links that might be helpful to their information-gathering efforts (even if it is unrelated to McDonalds).

Why? Rick Wion, the leader of the company's social media efforts told me that when McDonalds decides to host an event and invite these bloggers, every one of them will have a friend at McDonalds. That's a company that "gets it." Building deep and meaningful human relationships ... one small interaction at a time.

So a critical foundation of social media is providing consistent, meaningful provocations to remind customers that you are there, you love them, and you want to help them. This is really the first time in history businesses have had the chance to do this on a mass scale!

Now let's peel the onion back another layer and start to explore not only the "why" but the "how."

Questions leaders need to consider

1. If a series of consistent, small, meaningful provocations can lead to customer connection and perhaps even loyalty, what would that look like in my industry? What kind of provocations would engage our customers? What social media platforms could potentially deliver this "drip, drip, drip" of communications?

2. How are our competitors approaching this? How can we do this better than them? Is this an opportunity to create a distinctive experience for our customers?

3. Are customer service experiences with our company positive or negative "provocations?" Are we creating advocates for our brand or potential terrorists for our brand when we handle complaints?

4. How is every potential customer touch point a provocation? How can we turn touch points into trust points that encourage deeper engagement with our company?

Chapter Three

The social media mindset

Every time we have a new technology available to us, we tend to force our old habits onto it.

For example, when we started making movies, we simply filmed plays at first because that's what we were accustomed to.

When radio came on the scene, the first broadcasting pioneers recruited vaudeville stars like Jack Benny or Milton Berle to perform on the air because that is the type of entertainment we were conditioned to expect.

And I can remember, as a young marketer, helping to create our company's first website by handing the web developer what? Brochures! We simply took the same copy and photos from the brochures and created our new website! Of course websites grew and matured to represent so much more but the adoption of new technology certainly repeated this pattern, didn't it?

The same is true today. We have grown to love broadcasting, advertising, and press releases and that is what many companies are shoving through their social channels. Their approach to the social web is "A-ha! Another place for us to advertise!" And they routinely fail.

To be successful in this most human of channels, with this historic opportunity to create consistent, small provocations that lead to engagement and loyalty, we must adopt a new mindset. The Social Media Mindset.

I explore this topic extensively in *The Tao of Twitter* (in fact this mindset IS the Tao of Twitter!) but it really applies to any approach to social media.

If you're already a fan of The Tao, you have my permission

to skim this chapter, but if you haven't read this book, pay close attention because this may be the most important chapter in the book!

Behind every successful social media case study, behind every success story, you will find these three elements without fail:

Targeted Connections

+

Meaningful content

+

Authentic Helpfulness

=

Business Benefits

Let's take a trip to Wales

To explain this Social Media Mindset, let me rely on the help of a friend I made through the Internet named Tony Dowling, a business executive who lives in Wales.

Tony is an established and successful leader in the Welsh media industry but he knew that to be successful in the digital age, he simply had to understand, and master, social media. More than anyone, Tony knew the value of traditional media but he rapidly came to appreciate the value of this new mindset.

In an email to me introducing himself, here's what he had to say about this subject:

I read The Tao of Twitter *and was immediately inspired. As a media owner I like to keep up with the changes in the world of marketing, advertising, and communications, so I devour books like "Tao" and regularly, but never has one struck me so deeply and so quickly.*

I had a flash of inspiration — a genuine, physical feeling — that hit me around the part of the book that talks about "authentic helpfulness." I decided that I was going to try to follow this path, to stop selling and be selfless ... to give back to the universe.

I was going to start out in social media, build a blog, and use Tao as my guide.

I decided to blog about what I know, and freely give away all the knowledge I had. My blog is literally called "Completely Free Marketing Advice." I put my heart into it and created a lot of content quickly — a collection of my thoughts about selling, advertising, and marketing. Readers started to appear, as if by magic.

Using techniques lifted directly from the book, I slowly built an audience for the blog through Twitter and that audience started to become a community, becoming more involved in the discussions.

At first, many of my existing contacts I had built using the Tao came forward and asked for help. Then, they started to encourage others to join in. After only a few dozen blogs I had a group of regulars and around 15 new "clients" forming a community around "Completely Free Marketing Advice."

What amazed me the most, is the almost perfect predictions the book makes about the journey I have undertaken.

Over the months, word continued to spread, through Twitter of course, and Facebook too. And now readers are connecting through my words and are beginning to help each other! Everyone is taking part. The authentic helpfulness is spreading, and so are the business benefits.

The people following the blog are slowly but surely melding into a genuine community — interested only in helping each other out. Some of these people have become my good friends, people who have challenged me, and inspired me through their own authentic helpfulness.

Tony and I became great friends and that led to numerous collaborations and new business connections. Let's dissect Tony's success story piece by piece and uncover the three essential elements of the social media mindset.

Targeted Connections

No amount of work, time, or dedication to marketing and social media networking will work if you haven't surrounded yourself with people who might be interested in you and what you have to say.

While it might seem like there was an aspect of randomness to Tony's success, the conditions were ripe for these connections because he systematically surrounded himself with people likely to want to know him, learn from him, and help him.

This is the aspect of social media success that most companies miss. They understand the need to create some kind of content in the form of Facebook posts, tweets or blog posts, but they ignore the fact that behind every social media success, there has to be both a content strategy and a network strategy.

Purposefully, systematically, and continuously building your relevant network is essential because your content isn't going to work for you if it isn't ignited through your network ... and beyond. Amplification, after all, comes from size: The more followers or fans a business has, the more people who will see a message and who will, potentially, share it — and, thus, the more people who will potentially act on it.[1]

Before we move on, let me take this opportunity to moderate your expectations about this new audience you are building. Social media connections are normally "weak links" that are difficult to move toward action. Remember, our goal is to make connections and build loyalty and engagement over time ... with the keyword being "time."

---

[1] If you are interested in this, I write about this idea comprehensively in the book Return On Influence.

Social networks are effective at increasing participation—by lessening the level of motivation that participation requires. It takes no effort to click a "like" button, for example. But it takes more investment to actually act on a person's influence and buy a book, show up at your store, or contribute to a charity.

In his much-debated *New Yorker* article "Small Change," Malcom Gladwell noted that the Facebook page of the Save Darfur Coalition has 1,282,339 members, who have donated an average of nine cents apiece. The next biggest Darfur charity on Facebook has 22,073 members, who have donated an average of thirty-five cents. Help Save Darfur has 2,797 members, who have given, on average, fifteen cents. A spokesperson for the Save Darfur Coalition told *Newsweek*, "We wouldn't necessarily gauge someone's value to the advocacy movement based on what they've given. This is a powerful mechanism to engage this critical population. They inform their community, attend events, volunteer. It's not something you can measure by looking at a ledger."

In other words, Facebook activism succeeds not by motivating people to make a real sacrifice but by motivating them to do the things that people do when they are not motivated enough to make a real sacrifice. Like click their mouse on a "like" button.

This is a complicated issue that might vary by personality, industry, and subject matter. But my point is, as a leader, you must have realistic expectations about what can actually be accomplished through your company's social media audience and you should be wary of any consultant promising to deliver big results in a short period of time.

Meaningful Content

Think about your new social media fans and followers like atoms flying around the inside of a chemist's test tube, bumping into each other randomly. Obviously the more atoms you have in the tube, the better your chances that a reaction will occur! But every chemical reaction needs a catalyst, and on the social web, that catalyst is content.

Content has such an important role as the economic engine of the social web that it will get its own chapter later in this book, but let's look at the role it played in Tony's story.

Before the book, the story really began with Tony finding me. Because I work hard to develop meaningful content on my blog {grow}, it has earned me a place on a number of "best of" lists. It was one of these lists that led Tony to begin following me on Twitter, and eventually, it led him to my blog.

So my content helped create a reputation that landed me on a list, my tweets attracted Tony to my richer content, and he became a fan of my blog.

My blog content provided the small daily interactions that eventually led to a bigger interaction – Tony was interested enough in me to buy my book! Through *The Tao of Twitter*, Tony was inspired to create his own content through a new blog that attracted an entirely new audience that began to contribute their own business benefits.

Without content fueling the engine, none of this would have occurred! More on that in Chapter 5.

Authentic Helpfulness

In general, people go to sites like Facebook and YouTube to get away from the world. They want to see family photos, chat with friends, or view "Gangnam Style" for the tenth time. They probably don't want to hear about your new company ball caps or your new Chamber of Commerce award for community involvement.

But people do want to connect with companies and individuals who will help them make money, save money, have more fun and live a healthier life. The key to Tony's success came from pivoting his strategy from "selling" to "helping" and literally giving away everything he knew about business and marketing. I know this sounds strange and counter-intuitive but it really works.

A few months ago, I was approached by an entrepreneur who wanted to create a premium, paid content site for small business advice.

"This will be a place where you can reveal your very best ideas," he said.

"But I already do that on my blog," I explained. "I give away all my best ideas for free."

"No, I mean the best stuff you hold back for clients," he said.

"You're not understanding," I said, "I don't hold anything back. I give everything to my readers."

"Then how do you make any money?"

Giving it all away

I can understand why this is so puzzling. And yet, it works, and I do make money by giving away everything I know.

On the right hand side of my blog there is an item called "Categories" where you can peruse hundreds of blog posts by topic. So, for example, under the category of "blogging best practices," you can view more than 130 posts. I also have a free blogging eBook available and have done numerous podcasts and webinars on blogging … all completely free.

In a couple of hours, you can probably learn every idea and concept I have ever had about blogging. And yet, somebody calls me every single week willing to pay for blog coaching. I do social media workshops on content creation with huge companies like AT&T, Johnson & Johnson, and IBM. I give speeches on the topic all the time. And lots of folks are still buying *Born to Blog*, a book I co-wrote with Stanford Smith .

This doesn't even make sense, does it? How can I still make money dispensing blogging advice when I am giving away every blogging tip and secret I have ever had?

Business relationships are built on trust. They always have been. But for centuries we were limited by time and geography. We could only create trust with those who actually knew us, and probably within a relatively small area.

The social web is an incredible gift to businesses everywhere. For the first time in history, we can create relationships and build trust with people far and wide … through our voice, our views, our expertise. But the only way to do that is by unlocking and unleashing our content in a selfless and helpful way.

Even though I give away everything I know about business and marketing, people are still eager to hire me because they value my perspective and they trust me through the content I provide. What kind of content could you give away?

- Case studies
- White papers
- eBooks
- Newsletters
- Videos
- Slide presentations
- Recipes

- Stories
- Instructions
- Photographs
- Infographics
- Podcasts
- Reviews

The possibilities are endless.

When I started my consulting business, I took all the business I could get on a regional level. Slowly my business evolved and grew -- completely on the back of my blog content. And now I have made connections all over the world through social media. In fact, I have never spent one dime on any form of advertising for my business so far.

In other words, my business has grown ONLY because I give everything away!

I know this sounds counter-intuitive but being generous with your ideas is the key to eCommerce today. Not only do you create an inbound audience, you have an unprecedented opportunity to establish authority and trust, probably far beyond your normal sales "territory."

Unlock your content. Unleash it. And watch your business grow!

The social media mindset in action

To complete the story of Tony Dowling, giving away his content and building trust with his audience was like attaching jet propulsion to his business. Day by day, Tony reported on his increasing successes and I finally suggested (through a tweet) that he should create a social media conference in Wales to gather this wonderful community together. "We'll do it!" he said.

Within 24 hours he had 10 volunteers, an outline for an agenda, and his first sponsor. Within three days he had a venue (the amazing Celtic Manor Resort), funding from the Welsh government, and his first guest speaker – me. There was no way I was going to miss the world's first Tao of Twitter Conference. This conference led to additional business connections for me that created these tangible benefits for my business:

- A new regular writer for my blog

- A connection with a powerful venture capitalist in Dublin

- An invitation to keynote an annual conference in Ireland

- A company purchased 1,200 copies of my book *Return On Influence*

- I received an invitation to give a speech before an influential European Think Tank

- The Bank of Ireland paid me to do a workshop at their office

- IBM hired me to do a series of speeches for their employees in London

Remember how all this started. The genesis was giving away my content in an authentic and helpful way.

Do you believe that at any time in this evolving relationship my aim was to sell my professional services to Tony? I hope you replied "no"... and if you did you're on your way to understanding this very crucial aspect to the new media marketing mindset.

It's a bit unnerving to think "help, help, help" people instead of "sell, sell, sell" to people, but it really works.

In an always-on, real-time, global world of business

communications, the priority is on human interaction that leads to connections. Connections lead to awareness. Awareness leads to trust. Trust is the ultimate catalyst to business benefits, as it always has been.

Let's keep building on our foundation as we turn to the fourth element of social media strategy – The Information Eco System.

Questions leaders need to consider

1. What are the ways our business can systematically and continuously build our audience of relevant connections? Do we know where are our customers are getting their information today?

2. If we think beyond the company news releases, how can we create content that is really useful to our customers? What content do we already have at our company that can be re-purposed for social media sites like Facebook, YouTube and Twitter?

3. How can we be even more helpful to our customers? Can we distinguish ourselves in this way by using social media to reach and help customers in new ways?

4. What part of our corporate culture would enable this change in mindset? What is going to hold us back? What is my role in preparing us for success?

Chapter Four

The information eco-system

Let's now build upon a few of the concepts we've covered:

- For many people, the social web is replacing traditional media as a form of education, news, product discovery, and entertainment.

- Social media's place in this new marketing mix is to provide human, consistent, small provocations through various forms of content to ignite engagement and create loyalty over time.

- This can only be accomplished by adopting a Social Media Mindset based on creating targeted connections, meaningful content, and authentic helpfulness.

The fourth concept is a simple one. If more and more people are spending time on the social web, and they are looking for products and services there, then you need to be there too.

Your company needs to systematically populate the social web with content that interrupts them along their journey and directs them, eventually, back to your website. Although visits to traditional websites are also down for many companies, their importance remains because this is where a lot of your business gets done.

Today, Google is the "800 number" of the Internet. Type in a question, get an instant answer. So if somebody is picking up "the phone" and asking about your products and services, who is answering? Your competitor? Somebody who has written a review about your company? Somebody who loves you? Somebody who hates you?

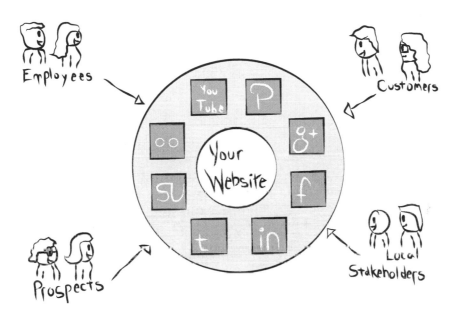

You would hope it would be YOU answering the question, right? And for that to happen, you need to show up in the first three search results on Google, if possible. Depending on your industry, this can be extremely difficult. If you're selling smartphones nationwide, this is going to be a very competitive and expensive space. But for many businesses, you might be surprised how inattentive the competition is. With a comprehensive social media strategy and some well-placed content in this information eco-system, you may be on your way to increasing brand awareness and inbound leads from the web.

This practice of "search engine optimization" or SEO, is very complex, and as you might imagine, the stakes are very high. A multi-billion-dollar industry has emerged to work on nothing more than improving search results! Plowing this ground is far beyond the scope of this book but if you want to learn more, I recommend Lee Odden's book *Optimize* as an excellent primer.

Google has continued to tweak its process to favor businesses who are trying to create helpful, organic, high-quality content for their customers. So an aggressive content plan can work wonders in this environment.

Think of the social media platforms like Facebook, Twitter and LinkedIn in a circle surrounding our website. The role of the website is like a subway station, shuttling people to wherever they need to go to get the information they need about our company. And if people first find us on the social web, the "outer circle," then we need to eventually nudge them back to the middle – to our website where we have our products and calls to action.

How do we get started?

A very easy and effective strategy is to brainstorm every question your customers could possibly have about your products, services, repairs, locations, benefits, and company in general ... and then answer them. That way when people are searching for an answer, they are more likely to find you.

Consistent, helpful content that answers these questions might be in the form of a blog post, a video, or even a FAQ or case study. We'll get into content strategy a little more in the next chapter.

Content Marketing

One of the hot buzzwords around now is "content market-ing." It's not rocket science and the idea isn't really new. Content marketing not only focuses on the type of content a customer might need, but also *when* they need it. There may even be differ-ent content plans for different types of buyer personas, different market verticals, and different regions of the world.

This may sound complicated but here's an easy exercise to unearth content marketing opportunities for your company. Take all the questions that you're going to answer from the previous section and plot those against the stages in your sales funnel. If you

Weeeeeee

LEADS

HOT LEADS

PROSPECTS

CUSTOMERS

answered those questions, which ones would help people in the early stages of the buying process? What if they are comparing you to the competitors? Do they have the answers they need in the form in which they need it to tilt the sale toward you?

Once you have the customer, what content do you need to have available to build their loyalty, answer their service questions, and teach them how to best utilize your products and services? Can you create content that actually rewards your best customers?

That's the basic idea of content marketing – Connect your customers to useful content at each stage in the purchasing process.

A Content Marketing Case Study

Let's look at an example of how one small company did this effectively. I like this case study because using the concepts I've laid out so far, a clever marketer was able to overcome an extremely difficult marketing challenge.

The first difficulty is that the business in this case is a medical clinic, so there are regulatory and patient privacy considerations. Second, it's a clinic that provides cosmetic surgery – not normally a "conversational topic" you might plaster all over a Facebook page. And finally, this example occurred during an extremely difficult economic period. How do you sell an expensive elective surgery in a recession, especially with tough competition?

That is one tall marketing mountain to climb ... unless of course you possess the business savvy of the clinic's business manager, Lisa Reath. A few years ago, Lisa took my social media marketing class and simply caught fire with new ideas. "I realized that I needed to stop selling so much and just be helpful and available," she said. "That was a new mindset for me and our business. We decided to create content that was authentically helpful."

The first thing the clinic did was brainstorm all the questions their clients could possibly have about their services. In addition to blogging about these issues (which helped SEO enormously), Lisa posted the question on their Facebook page each Wednesday as a poll. Then on Friday, the doctor answered the question on a simple, home-made video that was posted to both YouTube and Facebook. They also promoted the quiz, and the answer video on Twitter. So by using this "answer the questions" strategy, they were able to populate four different points in the information eco-system with one piece of content: their blog, Facebook page, YouTube account and Twitter feed. The rich content of the video was the engine behind the entire social media strategy.

"Given the privacy expectations with plastic surgery, we have had surprising success with Facebook," Lisa said. "It's largely because of a quiz game we play every week with our fans. We came up with the 'Truth-O-Meter' to establish ourselves as an authority and sort through all the misconceptions surrounding plastic surgery."

After Dr. Reath answers the weekly question, a winner is randomly chosen from the correct answers on the Facebook poll and anounced by a short YouTube video. Prizes include gift cards, skin care products, and contributions to charity in honor of breast cancer awareness month. To claim prizes, participants had to visit the clinic, so it drove foot traffic to their store and gave them a chance to meet their fans in real life.

It took a few months for the content strategy to kick in, but then the results started to accumulate week by week. In fact the effort was so successful, Lisa began to think about what else they could do populate the information eco-system with even more helpful content. It occurred to her that many potential clients might be shy about participating in the Q&A so she created another connection point: a high-quality eBook.

"I think our most successful marketing effort is a 33-page Girlfriend's Guide to Breast Augmentation," she said. "It is designed to be read online or on an iPad, downloaded free, easily forwarded and linked to.

"Our idea was to offer patients free information about breast augmentation that is helpful but not easily found online. Chapters are informative but also entertaining. We went out of our way to try not to directly sell our practice."

The publication became so popular that other medical practices wanted to buy the eBook to distribute to their own patients.

Let's look at the results. After one year of consistent content publication, here are a few highlights:

- The clinic reversed declining revenue and in spite of a severe recession, actually increased revenue 19%.

- Conversion rate for prospects visiting the clinic went from 55% to 70% because "Patients feel they know us and come in ready to schedule."

- The clinic had 2,082 Facebook fans with more than 200 regularly engaging in contests.

- Nearly 10,000 downloads of the Girlfriend's Guide eBook.

- 110% increase in referrals to the website from Facebook.

- Top ranking for all key search terms – without spending any money on SEO!

Not only did the search engine success drive new awareness within the clinic's target geographic area, it attracted new business from many other parts of the country. These customers were "calling the 800 number" and Lisa's clinic answered their call!

The principles outlined here can be applied to almost any business. Of course the real source of the success is content, an element of social media success that is so important it deserves its own chapter. Let's dive in!

Questions leaders need to consider

1. What social media platforms should be in our "information eco-system?"

2. Should we limit our efforts at first to concentrate on the social media platforms most likely to deliver results? Do we have the appropriate skills and resources to do that?

3. What metrics would we use to determine if we are connecting to our customers in the right places?

4. Do we expect the social media platforms in our information eco-system to change over time? How do we prepare for this? How do we know when to shift?

Chapter Five

Content is the Catalyst

If the social web were a living organism, content would be the air that it breathes.

"Content" has been bobbing and weaving in and out of the first four chapters of this book and yet there is so much more to learn if we are to understand the inner workings of social media strategy. Content is not merely a means to an end or a line item on a budget. Content is a revolution in how we think about power and influence in the business world.

Content is power

In the traditional carbon-based world, there are several ways to acquire power. You might have a position on an organizational chart. You may have a degree from an important university like Oxford or Harvard. Perhaps you control scarce resources like food, gold or oil. It's even possible to be powerful just by looking powerful! If somebody walks up to you wearing a police uniform, you're going to pay attention, right?

But the Internet is an entirely different place. Nobody cares about that stuff. Nobody knows where you went to school or how much money you have. Nobody cares what you look like or what car you drive. So how does one acquire power in the world with no titles or organizational charts? In a place that hates rules and authority? In an environment where you never quite know who is whom?

And yet, without question, people do become powerful on the Internet, and perhaps only on the Internet. How?

While some of these traditional notions of real-world influence still show up on the Internet, there is another force at work, a historic opportunity propelled by two parallel technological enablers: widespread access to high-speed Internet and free, easy-to-use publishing tools such as Twitter, Facebook and blogging. And that, of course, is the ability to publish content that gets shared throughout your network and beyond.

In my book *Return On Influence* (McGraw Hill, 2012), I explore this issue in detail and describe implications of this trend. I think it's important to review a few highlights from this book in the context of what it means to your business.

First and foremost is the power to become an influencer yourself, whether you are a person, a business, or a brand. If you follow the foundational strategies laid out in this book, you have an opportunity to create a voice of authority that can reach more broadly than ever before possible.

In a personal example, I wrote one single blog post a few years ago that ended up getting me prominently featured in the *New York Times*, the *London Daily Mail*, and the *CBS Morning News*. How would that have been possible even five years ago? It would not be. This is a revolutionary time to be able to spread your influence far and wide ... and perhaps at very low cost. What would that kind of advertising exposure have cost me a few years ago?

Not all content is created equal

Let's summarize the business benefits of this one particular blog post:

- Writing the post helped clarify my thinking on a subject and create useful content for my readers.

- The content spread virally, attracting thousands of new people to my site and my business.

- Comments on the blog provided me with lots of new ideas and helped create another idea for something bigger — a book.

- Since the original content was shared so much, it helped influence Google's search results, which helped attract the attention of a reporter from a very important newspaper, resulting in millions of impressions for my personal brand in newspapers around the world.

Now here is the key question to consider. Would any of this had happened if I had only posted my thoughts on the subject through a Facebook post, a tweet, or a LinkedIn update? Of course not. I needed to provide rich content to have a chance at benefits like this.

There is no guarantee something like this will happen to you if you create original, rich content. But I do guarantee it will never happen if you don't.

One common mantra we all hear over and over again is "content is king."

And this is true, but not just any content will do. A link, a funny photo, a famous quote, or even a recipe or coupon are legitimate types of content, but these are not the types of content that will optimize your social media presence and bring you powerful, lasting results. To really go for it, you must have at least one source of original rich content and you probably have just three viable options:

A blog.

A podcast.

A video series.

Only in-depth, conversational content from at least one of these sources will provide the content fuel to give you a chance to reap the immense benefits from a social media strategy.

There are other possible secondary sources — photographic content, Slideshare presentations, perhaps a Pinterest page — but the three tried and true sources accessible to most businesses are blogs, podcasts, and video.

Once you make that decision and begin to execute, you'll have the content available to power whatever social media platforms you choose. A source of rich content provides something that is then shareable, conversational, and engaging for Facebook, Twitter, LinkedIn, and other social platforms.

After you have a solid business and marketing strategy in place, and you are ready to embark on this wonderful social media journey, I suggest your first question should be, "What is the source of my rich content?"

Content and word of mouth influence

Another opportunity embedded in this content trend is the unprecedented ability to find those powerful word of mouth influencers who may be advocates for our brand or message through their own content. We've always known that certain "super connectors" can help spread the word and validate your product or service. But it used to be difficult and expensive to find these people. That has all changed.

Today, complex mathematical algorithms have been developed that can identify who is out there creating, sharing and spreading content by any topic imaginable ... in other words, we can easily find the people skilled at creating online buzz about our products.

In an example from *Return On Influence,* Turner Broadcasting used a company called Klout to identify individuals influential in "science fiction" and "television" to help launch a new series called "Falling Skies." This allowed the network to reach out and connect with people who would be likely enthusiasts of the new show – and people they had never even heard of before.

Throughout the season, TBS provided various little incentives to make this group of influencers feel special and rewarded for their interest and loyalty. The results were dramatic. By the end of the season, 60 percent of the entire volume of Internet content was being directly or indirectly generated by this small band of enthusiasts. This buzz correlated to brand awareness and even higher advertising revenues.

But something even more interesting happened. The group of influencers became aware of each other and formed their own community around the television program. They became friends and formed an emotional connection to the television show. When the season was over, they wanted to know what they could do to continue to create buzz through the summer until the next season.

One of the pioneers in this field of influence marketing is Azeem Azhar, founder of a company called PeerIndex that attempts to identify these influencers.

"The old channels of creating influence were quite clear -- and dysfunctional," he said. "In order to have impact, you needed to go to the right university ... check that box ... get a job with the right newspaper or investment bank ... check that box ... and guess what? Now you have influence.

"But actually, it's not influence," Azhar said. "It's hurdle jumping. You're jumping the hurdles of your SAT, your GRE, GMAT, or other entrance exams. You're jumping the hurdle of the late night drink with the city editor of the local paper or investment banker who you're hoping is going to recruit you. That was the old way to get ahead and get noticed.

"But we found some really smart people hanging around in this social space with no clear metric to distinguish who you should trust, and on what subject. We knew that within the data on the social web there were some really clear indications of people's tendencies and behaviors. There were patterns that would indicate the topics that they really cared about ... and maybe even some indicators of influence on certain topics.

"A powerful analogy for this is the personal credit rating. In that case, a corporate entity looks at all of the previous activity for a person going back five or 10 years and sums it up in a single number. A smart loan officer will dig through the details to make the best assessment, but if you need a quick decision, that single number will probably work. That's the type of metric we're trying to provide around influence. The idea of using influence in business has come a long way, but we are just at the beginning of understanding and measuring this science of influence."

The content arms race

There are tens of thousands of executives just like you trying to figure out social media and they're all coming to the same conclusion: We need to step up our content efforts.

To succeed on the social web today you need to consistently provide useful, relevant, and entertaining content — and that is not cheap. And as the information density on the web increases, so too will the cost to produce that great content. Don't be lulled into thinking social media marketing is "free." It's not.

In fact, the Physics of Social Media is working against you every day. Now, don't freak out. It's not complicated or boring, and it makes no mention of black holes or the Higgs Boson. It's a pretty simple but important idea about the increasing demands on your content and marketing messages. Let's look at the two colliding factors that will dramatically impact your marketing initiatives.

1) The amount of available information is accelerating. I recently saw an infographic reporting that all of the information created in the past two years equals the amount of recorded information for all of human history. We are in a permanent state of information overload and it's going to get much, much worse.

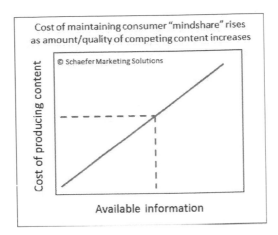

2) Our processing capability is the same. We only have one brain that evolved to process basic threats, physical needs, and verbal communication. The physics of the human brain is woefully unprepared for this information onslaught. We cannot add processing speed to that limited capacity (at least yet).

In the physical world, this is what happens when you try to push too much stuff though a finite pipeline — catastrophic failure. A flood. Wires bursting into flame. Servers crash.

So this presents the fundamental dilemma for you and me. How do we get our marketing message to cut through the dense fog of information and make it through to a consumer brain — without going broke or having a catastrophic strategic failure?

Three ways to maintain content mindshare

How do you fend for your piece of your customer's mindshare in the face of this information tsunami? There are only three possible strategies:

1) Maintain mindshare through increasingly spectacular content. This is the classic — but theoretically unsustainable — content marketing strategy: Offer amazing, useful content that will make people want to spend time with you. But the cost of maintaining this quality level is inexorably multiplying. This approach will inevitably stall as costs rise and companies discover economic value of loyalty.

2) Maintain "mindshare" with less pipeline. If the cost of maintaining mindshare is going to keep expanding (and it will), another idea is to find a way to push out the same amount of value through less time with your content. This would explain the meteoric rise of content curation, infographics, and visually-oriented sites like Pinterest and Instagram.

People don't have to read. They are capturing information quickly through images and moving on to the next item in the pipeline. I think it is safe to predict that we are just at the beginning of this trend.

3) Infiltrate other content with your message. This is like a Trojan Horse. When a consumer opens up somebody else's content they find you. The idea is that you let other content providers bear the huge cost of maintaining mindshare and you sneak in by "borrowing" their pipeline. Examples:

- Guest posts on popular sites

- Influencer outreach — Nurturing relationships with high-impact influencers willing to share and validate your content

- News-jacking — Establishing a voice of authority so that the news channels come to you.

- PR — Methodically finding opportunities to place content in big "pipelines"

I would suggest that a successful long-term social media marketing strategy must have at least parts of all three of these, in addition to an aggressive network building strategy.

If you made it this far, thank you. Together, we have now completed the section on the fundamentals of social media strategy. Now let's look at some of the toughest questions you're likely to have about social media marketing and clobber them head-on.

Upward, Onward!

Questions leaders need to consider

1. What are our existing sources of content that could be leveraged across the social web?

2. How are our competitors using content on the Internet? Is this field getting saturated?

3. What is our company's best source of rich content? A blog? A video? A podcast? Or something else?

4. How would a content marketing strategy affect our current resources and how would we adjust?

Section Two

The five most difficult questions you'll face

Chapter Six

What is the value of social media and how do we measure it?

Some variation of the "What is the ROI of social media" question is by far the most frequent topic in my university classes and corporate workshops. The answer is not elusive, but it does require a different mindset to understand the full potential of what is realistic, and what is possible.

Let's break it down and answer this important question on several levels, starting with the most basic premise ...

You must measure

I was speaking on a panel for Social Media Week in New York City when one of my fellow panelists said "This ROI stuff is just a bunch of crap. I'm so tired of it. You can't measure what you're doing and people should not even try."

I began to twitch.

"I agree," said the second panelist. "Too much focus is placed on measurement."

My head began to throb.

"As a social media marketer, I can't measure what I do," said the moderator. "I just do it."

At that point, the dam broke.

"Respectfully," I began, "I disagree with everything that has just been said! As marketers we should measure EVERYTHING. And generally, we can."

And it kind of went downhill from there. This dialogue is nothing new. It is merely a symptom of an anti-measurement bias upheld by many popular pundits and consultants.

My first warning is, if a consultant or employee comes to you suggesting that you don't have to measure your social media efforts, politely show them the door.

Here are four reasons why you MUST measure the results of your corporate social media activities.

1) There is an implied value to everything. At some point in the life of every company, there will be a financial imperative to slash overhead costs. The bubble always bursts, at least in a free economy. When that happens, everything will be evaluated under the icy glare of number-crunchers — do we cut or not cut?

This is the day of reckoning that defines the "implied economic value" of any program. Yes, the social media marketing effort will come under scrutiny. So will the receptionist, your wireless plan, and every other mundane daily activity not normally associated with an Excel spreadsheet. When it's your turn to justify the existence of your marketing efforts, you better be able to demonstrate business value, and it better be an explanation more convincing than "But our consultants said that we don't have to measure this!"

2) If we are expending human effort, it should be justified. Every economic activity in a corporation directly or indirectly has to contribute to shareholder value or eventually it will go away.

Let's look at how "un-free" social media really is. Let's assume you have one person working full-time on social media marketing. We'll assign that person a salary of $60,000. In a typical company, standard health, 401(k) and other benefit costs equal another 50 percent of the base salary, or in this case, $30,000. We'll assign another 20 percent of base salary for overhead such as office space, shared services support, and technology. That's $12,000. We won't even address travel, training, or bonuses.

So, our minimum full-up cost for one social media professional is $102,000. As a business owner, are you willing to spend more than $100,000 per year without requiring any accountability for a return?

3) If you're not measuring, how do you know you're making progress? Measurement provides a leading indicator to let you know if more or less resources should be expended on your efforts.

4) There is no excuse not to measure. If you have been in marketing for a while, you may have counted billboards, brochures, and trade shows in your traditional marketing mix.

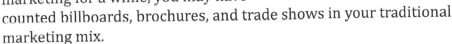

Have you ever tried to calculate the ROI of a billboard?

Here's the good news. Today, there is so much data flying at us that there really is no excuse NOT to measure your digital marketing activities.

Even a free program like Google Analytics can provide an extremely rich analysis of who is visiting your site, how much time they are spending there, where they abandon your site, what content is working the best for you, and countless other insights.

So if you were satisfied with the ability to measure your old marketing programs, you should be thrilled with the ability to measure your social media initiatives, right?

Using measurement as an excuse for inaction

My friend Matt Ridings of Sidera Works provided a very wise insight on my blog. "You should always measure," he said, "unless you shouldn't."

Here is what he meant by this observation ...

1) Spreadsheets should never be a substitute for business instincts. Too many fall back on spreadsheets as a means to avoid risk and accountability. Using ROI is an excuse not to move forward with something they don't understand.

2) Sometimes there is no ROI to measuring ROI. Just because something "can" be measured doesn't mean it "should" be measured. If the cost of trying to measure an activity outweighs the gain of the activity itself, or eats too far into that gain, then why would you measure it? It doesn't mean there was no gain, it means you have to make a decision based on more than spreadsheets as to whether you can mentally correlate enough benefit to quantify the activity to continue doing it.

3) Understanding appropriate time horizons and objectives is critical. Numbers mean nothing if you aren't balancing them against proper expectations. If you don't have a solid, educated theory as to how long an activity should take before it starts showing its full benefits (in a relationship driven economy the long tail activity becomes the norm so this becomes even more critical)

then how can you know when to make a decision to stop or increase that activity?

4) Understanding the impact of measurement, both positive and negative, is also critical. Measurement itself impacts the behaviors and decisions inside the organization. How does the measurement motivate or impact the individuals? Does it do so in ways that are beneficial to the customer or in ways that benefit the company in the short term but cuts its throat in the long term? In summary, it's not whether you measure, it's whether you understand what to do with it.

Now, let's look at an even more radical concept. Maybe the correct measures for your social media program are not expressed by any numbers at all.

The importance of qualitative measures

In the past 12 months, here are just a few of the business benefits I received directly from my social media presence:

- An invitation to lecture at Oxford University

- Free content for my blog from writers in France, Belgium, Malaysia, Australia, England, Wales, Scotland, Ireland, and Germany

- An intern

- A book contract

- Free art for my blog, book, Twitter profile, and Facebook page

- Free car service for a week in London

- $6,000 in donations to my favorite charity

- A tour guide for a day in Estonia

- Speaking opportunities in Japan, India, Canada, Holland, and the UK

- An eBook for my blog on best digital marketing campaigns

- Advice on how to solve a technical problem with my blog

- A job for a friend

Now every single item on this list is a tangible, personal or business benefit. But how many could you easily express on a spreadsheet or a pie chart? Not many.

This is a key idea. Many benefits from the social web are qualitative, not quantitative. That's why small businesses may have an advantage over large corporations in the social space if there is not a mindset change about measurement.

Small business owners in the social media trenches can see their efforts paying off every day. But chances are in a big company, the boss holding the purse strings is two or three levels above the people actually doing the work and at some point she will ask: "What is the ROI of all this tweeting? I want my pie chart!"

And that's when things start to crumble.

Let's just look at one isolated social media opportunity – blogging. Here are examples of 25 (yes, 25!) tangible, legitimate, non-financial benefits of having a company blog:

- **SEO** — Having an active, relevant blog can provide a powerful impact on search engine ranking.

- **Point of differentiation** — If your competitors don't blog, this an opportunity to stand out in your niche.

- **Solidify your Point of View** — The act of blogging forces you to be clear on your company's position on issues. Doing research, fact checking, writing, and re-writing helps you understand a subject more fully.

- **Create a database of answers** — Blog about customer questions. Use links to those posts to save time when answering future questions.

- **Reward employees** — Shine a spotlight on brilliant employees by featuring their ideas and accomplishments on your blog.

- **Marketing integration** — Turn content from your blog into useful sales and marketing materials. Printed collateral is often a dead end, but through a blog post, customers can continue investigating and learning.

- **Re-purpose the content** — Your blog content can be cost-effectively re-purposed for newsletters, eBooks, and other publications.

- **Humanize your brand** — There is probably no more powerful and cost-effective way to show the "soft" side of your business than storytelling through a blog.

- **Sign of activity** — A current blog confirms that your website is updated and relevant.

- **PR** — Tweets and Facebook status updates probably aren't going to attract the attention of reporters. Helpful blog posts will.

- **Pre-populate business relationships** -- People want to engage with those they know, like, and trust. Writing online allows people to get to know you before they even meet you. Many companies are turning employees into blogging rocks stars to support marketing efforts.

- **Customer engagement** — Creating a dialogue with your customers can lead to powerful business benefits. Why not have customers contribute posts?

- **Solve problems** — Some companies are using their blogs to crowd-source technical problem solving.

- **New product development ideas** — A hot trend is using the blog platform to deliver new product and service ideas.

- **Voice of authority** — Is your company the industry leader? Demonstrate your voice of leadership on your blog.

- **Market segmentation** — Many companies (especially in high tech) have multiple blogs to reach customers by different interest, demographic or geography.

- **Identify advocates** — Blog readers may be among your brand's most powerful fans.

- **Constant customer connection** — Calling on customers is expensive. But a blog post can be a little "sales call" every week.

- **Test ideas** — Need to take a position? Why not test it with the blog community first?

- **Assemble chapters for a book** — Many companies piece together blog posts to create larger publications. This list originally appeared on my blog!

- **Research** — Throw a question out there and use your blog as a cost-effective and rapid way to get feedback.

- **Networking** – Blog connections can lead to finding interns, suppliers and partners.

- **Establish emotional connection** — Blogging's ability to connect through a story is powerful — especially for non-profits.

- **Social Proof** — Simply having a consistent blog sends a message that your company "gets" social media.

- **Crisis management** – If you have a blog, you don't have to rely on the press to get the story straight. Your blog can put the facts out there to defend your brand.

I could have developed a similar list of qualitative benefits for Facebook, Twitter, YouTube and every other social media platform. The companies most advanced in applying social media may be focusing completely on the qualitative benefits ...

- PepsiCo has used social networks to gather customer insights via its DEWmocracy promotions, which have contributed to the creation of new varieties of its Mountain Dew brand.

- Caterpillar uses social media to create communities and build loyalty by rewarding customers for helping other customers solve technical problems.

- Audi has used social media to research new "influencers" in the areas of design and technology to tap into entirely new potential market segments.

- A regional telecomm used its fanbase to crowd-source ideas on how to celebrate the company's 30th year in business.

- Citi uses social media to connect with high-potential job candidates.

- Starbucks has a blog devoted to collecting and sorting through ideas to improve their products and stores. They have implemented thousands of ideas while involving their biggest fans in the creation of their company.

If you're only focused on a quantitative measure like ROI, you're missing the boat on many of the most important benefits of social media marketing.

Creating Metrics that Matter

By now I hope you're getting an idea of the limitless possibilities of creating value through social media applications. Yet study after study shows that many companies are struggling with the value proposition of social media.

Why? I think that most of them are focused on the wrong measures.

A good place to start is to accurately define the behaviors and attitudes you are trying to influence through your social media presence, and then find the appropriate analytics that line up with those well-understood goals.

Social media accountability means delivering and demonstrating progress against the company's natural objectives. Whether quantitative or qualitative, the measurements need to be part of the building blocks of the reports, dashboards, and KPIs already familiar to the business.

What is ingrained in your company? Maybe your team thinks in terms of a sales funnel. Perhaps it is cost per registrant. Maybe the key goal is customer satisfaction or brand awareness. You have to show results in a manner that is relevant to the stakeholders' perspective.

Let's say your existing company goal is to increase customer loyalty. Relevant loyalty measurements would include number of comments and interactions, sign ups on sites, and the number of friends and followers. Individually, none of these items show loyalty, but looking at them collectively provides loyalty insights that can enhance your existing KPI's.

And while we're on the subject or measurement, I am going to put in a plug for rigorous statistical analysis. We have an unprecedented opportunity to distill true value and insight from the "big data" streaming at us through the social web. But accurate statistical analysis is almost completely lacking in this field right now.

As a leader, do not accept "eye-balling" the data. Real competitive advantage will come to the companies who can follow data, not hunches.

Keep it simple, but keep measuring

I want to end this chapter with some unconventional wisdom that I think will make sense to you, especially if you are trying get some traction in the early stages of a program.

Most consultants will be quick to point out that activity-based metrics such as number of posts, followers, or tweets are meaningless because they don't measure real business value. I'm going to take a contrarian view. In the real world, not only do they matter, they may be critical.

A few years ago, I was working as a consultant on a new marketing initiative for an extremely conservative, slow-moving company. As we were getting to know each other, I asked the people around the table "If we gathered here a year from now and you told me that our initiative had been wildly successful, what would have been achieved?"

One of the veterans of the team spoke up: "I would like to see that something … anything … actually HAPPENED!"
This may seem like a sad little tale, but don't you see this reluctance to change in so many companies?

This highlights a very important point: In the real world, sometimes CHANGE needs to be the business goal before you can start chalking up business benefits like leads or sales. In fact, a simple indicator of progress may be the most important goal you can possibly have for an early social media program.

You see, for a slow-moving company immersed in a digital transition, budget, resources, and a plan of action are not going to guarantee success if the company culture does not support the effort.

To lead an initiative that eventually creates business results, you need to have an effort that is active, sustained, and consistent. Early on, it's important to show that we are achieving an activity level — that SOMETHING is happening! That's why unpopular metrics such as posts per month, audience growth, or even number of "likes" may be absolutely critical to a fledgling effort in a conservative company.

The simple act of **forward progress** may be the most important goal of all, and a leading indicator of better things to come! Here are examples of simple metrics that can indicate rising activity levels and a company culture moving in the right direction:

- Number of employees actively posting

- Number of content posts per month

- Audience size (Facebook, Twitter, YouTube, etc.)

- Number of social mentions

- Number of blog/Facebook comments

- Number of departments participating

- Traffic to social sites

- Binary measures such as "did we create a Facebook page" a YouTube channel or a blog

- Did we attend social media training? Did we have an executive social media workshop?

While it is true that none of these would necessarily indicate an alignment with sales objectives, without consistent participation and a growing audience, you will never get to the point where finding business benefits is achievable. We have to walk before we can run.

There are four other benefits to these simple metrics.

1. It drives the right behavior in the organization at this early stage.

2. It is fairly easy to observe quick progress that leads to achievable milestones and momentum.

3. The metrics are very easy to collect and understand (compared to something like bounce rate or reach).

4. Finally, no matter how well you plan, you can never predict exactly what is going to happen once you go down this road. You may find unexpected benefits, and consequently unexpected new metrics, that illustrate your progress. Don't try to over-think everything up front. At some point, doing it is more important than planning it.

So if you're just starting out in a conservative company culture, I would encourage you to look for simple metrics that provide an indication of progress. There is no rule that says you can't add or change metrics nine months down the road as your initiative begins to mature.

In summary,

- Don't accept any advice counseling you to not measure your social media efforts.

- Consider your investment in social media activities in terms of "relevance" as well as ROI.

- Measure ROI when you can but sometimes that isn't practical. Don't let that stop you. There are plenty of other ways to measure your efforts and propel your marketing initiatives.

- The leading companies will recognize the value of qualitative, as well as quantitative measurements.

- The opportunities to create and quantify value through social media applications are limitless. In addition to sales, consider how cost savings, innovation, and internal applications of the technology are rich areas for creating business benefits.

- Aligning metrics with existing goals -- and in familiar terms -- will help demonstrate the value of your efforts.

- Don't overlook the power of simple measures that demonstrate forward progress.

Questions leaders need to consider

1. A year from now, what would a successful social media initiative look like?

2. With those goals in mind, what metrics are available that could indicate our progress?

3. Does our company have a culture that can acknowledge and embrace qualitative measures? What are the implications if we don't?

Chapter Seven

We're in a niche market. Do we really need to use social media?

■ ■ ■ **O**r, instead of "niche" substitute "B2B," "mature" or "declining."

This is a very common and legitimate question. Moving to a social media strategy is a big decision (and potentially an expensive one!) so you need to question it very carefully.

Let's start exploring this question with a cautionary tale from one of America's most dominant brands ... or at least it used to be.

I was driving home from a family vacation using an iPhone app called "Navigon." This is an excellent GPS and mapping application that gets me where I want to go without the expense and hassle of schlepping another device around.

I began to wonder ... why am I not using a mapping application from Rand McNally, the dominant market leader in all things maps for decades? For most of my life a well-worn copy of a *Rand McNally Atlas of the United States* book of maps was a fixture in my car. Can you even name another company that made U.S. road maps? Certainly, Rand was the gold standard for getting you to where you wanted to go.

So I did a little research. The company had a minor entry in the GPS device market and is usually grouped under the "other" category in the analyst reports. A search for Rand McNally in the iTunes app store delivers one sad little entry that allows you to "vote for the best small towns of 2011 — right from your mobile device!" For Android systems, there is nothing at all.

Sad. Sad. Sad.

I can imagine the conversation among the Rand McNally executives five years ago ... "Digital? Are you CRAZY? Do you know what the ROI is on our paper maps? Why in the world would we ever cut into that profit margin? Nobody seems to be able to demonstrate an ROI of digital maps!"

It's probably the same conversation that echoed through the halls of Kodak ... "But we make so much money on film! What is the ROI for sharing digital photos on the Internet? It's folly!"

I wonder what the ROI of bankrupt is?

So as you consider the question of how social media and digital marketing applies to your business: Do you risk becoming obsolete if you don't go digital?

And by digital, I don't mean "a website." In the last two years, 68 percent of the Fortune 100 companies had a year-over-year decline in their website page views. Why? Because people are not looking for you on websites any more (unless you work for Amazon, eBay or Etsy of course). For most companies, having a website is simply not enough these days.

Every business exists to create shareholder value. But please don't overlook the possibility of not even existing in two years because you are milking an Excel spreadsheet for all it's worth. There are lots of bright people out there that want your company to die. Be them, or hire them. Just don't hold on to old business models until the banks are nailing your door shut.

Don't be Rand.

Does every company need a social media strategy?

As the hype of social media begins to die down and companies re-evaluate their efforts with a steely-eyed look at the cost versus benefits, this a fair, but complex, question. Let's explore this important issue by taking a romp through some unusual case studies that stretch the boundaries of social media marketing thinking.

Depend Adult Diapers – Do you need a social media

strategy? It depends! Get it? Oh, never mind.

Depend, a Kimberly Clark brand, has no apparent social media offerings. With its typically geriatric customer base, the product website offers a fitting guide and coupons but no social media way to connect. A company not affiliated with the brand has set up a rogue Facebook site called "Depend's adult diapers." So Kimberly Clark probably should protect itself by nailing down as many name alternatives as they can on the most popular social media platforms.

Even this brand should consider at least a modest Facebook outpost because their future customers will certainly be there. Also, more and more people are using Facebook to search for brand information. At least one competitor, Poise, already has a Facebook page.

Coal – Why would you want a social media presence if you sell a commodity product? There is perhaps no product less differentiated than coal. In a tough business like that, you simply try to excel where you can by managing the supply chain properly, staying on top of trading trends, and focusing on low production costs.

Peabody Energy is the largest publicly-traded coal company in the world. It has an excellent, informative website, but virtually no social presence (a token Twitter account and a weak Facebook page).

Perhaps Peabody's strategy is to do whatever they can to *avoid* social media connection. Let's face it, any company that scrapes away pristine countrysides to mine a product that is a major contributor to air and water pollution is not necessarily part of a conversation that is shareholder-friendly. Coal is important to the world economy, but it can be a dirty, dangerous business that sparks a lot of emotion in people. Should we support coal energy? It is an argument that will never be settled, and one the industry probably can never win. If they had a significant social media presence, the debates and hater harpoons would be endless.

Instead, Peabody can provide financial support to trade organizations like American Coalition for Clean Coal, which has a significant social media footprint — more than 1 million YouTube views, a blog, and a meaningful presence on Twitter and Facebook.

Should a company avoid the cost of social media

conversation and move it to a trade association? That may be a viable strategy.

Playing cards – I play this little marketing mind game with myself. I pick a seemingly dull product and then imagine what their social media presence might be. Like playing cards. What can you really say about those for heaven's sake? They haven't changed for centuries. Turns out, quite a lot.

I opened a new pack of Bicycle playing cards and was delighted to see an extra card promoting their social media properties: Twitter, Facebook, YouTube. These sites are filled with excellent content for people who love card games, card tricks, and even card-related arts and crafts. There are tons of fan conversations going on for this ancient gaming product.

Bicycle is not a highly conversational brand but this notably non-digital product is finding interesting ways to create new conversations, and renewed relevance, with a digital audience.

Radioactive Waste Removal – You have to love a company with a tagline of "Providing radioactive waste services since 1952." Straight to the point. And so is US Ecology, a company specializing in one of the most demanding B2B services on earth.

The company has no social media presence with the exception of a short LinkedIn page. Let's think about their business model. Somebody has a radioactive mess on their hands. There is a well-known and short list of qualified and trained people to clean it up. The customer inquires to see who is available and asks them to get there fast. There probably isn't much of a negotiation.

Or perhaps US Ecology has some long-term contracts with companies who generate radioactive waste. You probably don't want to pinch pennies in that case, either.

If it doesn't need Facebook to generate demand or customer connection, does US Ecology need a social media presence to attract and retain employees? Apparently not. I actually met some of their workers a few months ago and they were happy to have the job. They are paid well and the hours are good. There is little employee turnover in their area of expertise.

If you were the marketing director for US Ecology would you spend money on a social media marketing program? Probably not.

The world's oldest company – Fonderia Pontificia Marinelli has been casting beautiful bronze bells continuously in the quiet Apennine Hills of Italy since the year 1000. It is one of the five oldest companies in the world and, in fact, they have been making their bells the same way throughout the centuries.

The bells of Fonderia Pontificia Marinelli toll in the important buildings of New York, Beijing, Jerusalem, South America and Korea. The family business currently employs 20 people, five of them named Marinelli. The company also has a small museum and hosts special events.

They have a basic website circa 2000 and no social media presence. That doesn't mean that their content is not being shared by social media savvy visitors from throughout the world, but the old ways seem to suit this family business best.

Fonderia Pontificia Marinelli has made it through wars, natural disasters, and economic calamities without fail. Can it keep going without a social media strategy? Would it taint the charm of this ancient institution if they were out trying to stir up Facebook Likes? If you are looking for an epic bronze bell, would you buy from this company, even if they didn't have a Twitter account?

Somehow, I think they will outlast us all.

Does every company need a social media strategy? Here is the question you need to answer first ...

Does it fit our current business strategy?

How do you know if your company is right for social media? Should you experiment, go all in, or simply show up?

The answer to that starts with a simple exercise. Can you finish this sentence?

"Only we ..."

This is probably the hardest task in all of business but it's absolutely essential because it unearths your points of differentiation, the nature of competition, the needs of your customers, and ultimately, your strategy. If you haven't considered this in a while, has it changed?

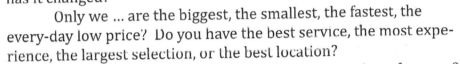

Only we ... are the biggest, the smallest, the fastest, the every-day low price? Do you have the best service, the most experience, the largest selection, or the best location?

Why do customers love you? Why do competitors fear you? What is it about you that keeps them coming back year after year? And if you think you know ... are you still sure? Are you sure you are aligned with customer needs? Are you continually improving and refreshing your core competencies?

Do you know where they are getting their information? Are they spending time on the social web at work? At home? Could this be a point of differentiation for your company?

If you haven't spent time considering the changing needs of your customers, it might be time to get out and talk to them or do a survey. While we're focused on serving, it is often difficult to see what's coming next.

If you can answer "only we" thoroughly, accurately, and confidently, it's likely that your marketing strategy will reveal itself. You'll know with certainty what you need to say and where you need to say it. You'll have a good idea how much the social web should be part of that strategy.

A few years ago, I helped a customer through an evaluation like this. Before we began the customer research, the owner and founder was sure that her customers (large national charities and foundations) were not using the social web and had no interest in it.

But when we asked her customers what they were worried about for the upcoming year, the number one answer, by far, was figuring out how to use social media. They knew their customers and donors were using it every day as an essential communication and connection tool and they needed to get on board fast.

My customer realized that she needed to get ahead of the curve and actually demonstrate a competency in this area. She had an opportunity to anticipate the customer's need articulated in this research and actually build a new competency into her service offerings. She immersed herself in blogging, Twitter and other connection points and eventually had enough skill to host webinars for her customers on effective social media use. Through social media, she was able to add a new "only we."

Are you watching for changing trends and innovations among your competitors? Even in the fragmented and highly-competitive field of social media marketing, there are certain over-arching themes emerging. Are you ahead of the curve or behind the curve? Do you even know?

Thinking about social media for the enterprise

In the first section of this book we went into detail about how social media can fit into a marketing strategy. Although this is usually the popular application of social media, it's not the only way to think about it for your company. There are other benefits, as well.

Public relations – It's likely that some aspect of social media has to be incorporated into any plan for media relations, crisis management, even planning and community relations.

Word of mouth advocacy – Social media opens up an entirely new way of identifying, and nurturing powerful online advocates for your brand.

Cost savings – Social media represents an extremely cost-effective communication channel. Most research shows that in terms of many traditional measures, the results are as good, or better, than paid advertising. There are many opportunities to leverage existing content and marketing materials across vast new audiences.

Customer service – You may not have a choice about this really. Social media has become a very popular way to complain about poor products and services. It's the new 800 number. Are you going to answer the call?

HR and recruiting – Social media, and particularly LinkedIn, has transformed the human resources function. One professional told me that a candidate's "social media footprint" was more important today than a resume! Whether you are trying to find talent or be found, social media is a critical piece of the puzzle.

Internal process improvement – In chapter 6, I discussed the vast potential of tapping into social media technologies to unleash employee productivity, collaboration, and problem-solving.

Reputation management – The largest brands have social media "war rooms" set up so they can monitor conversations and sentiment about their products and brands in real-time, at any spot in the world. Today, you need to be tuned-in to the conversations and respond quickly or risk problems going viral.

Research and development – An active customer community can be a goldmine of new ideas, and suggestions for products and innovations.

A word about regulated industries

There may be legitimate, legal reasons why you would not want to participate on the social web, especially if you're in an industry handling highly sensitive or confidential information.

Many companies in regulated industries like banking and pharmaceuticals are also struggling with establishing a presence on the social web.

The first rule of thumb is to listen to your Legal Department. Any organization dedicated to keeping me out of jail is very popular with me. Typically these folks will look for ways to help support the business and marketing efforts, so listen to their good counsel.

Having said that, my observation is that there are LOTS of

opportunities for regulated companies to participate on the social web and they simply use regulations as an excuse to do nothing because they simply don't understand or are afraid of change.

Some wealth management firms are so paranoid they don't even allow their advisors to have a LinkedIn account. One conversation with a wealth management advisor went like this:

"I'm really frustrated because my company does not allow us to use any social media platforms. They want to script everything we say. I feel like I am missing out."

"Do they allow you to attend chamber of commerce meetings to network?" I asked.

"Yes. I have gone to them for years."

"Do they give you a script about what to say and who to say it to?"

"No, of course not."

"Then what's the difference? Social media is just another way to network. In fact, it's the most powerful business networking tool ever created."

This conversation sufficiently inspired my friend to take my class. He became such an effective advocate of social media in his company that he was named to lead a committee to get the company on board and up to speed.

Likewise, there are many organizations in the healthcare field using social media extremely well. The Mayo Clinic, for example has dozens of popular blogs, an excellent YouTube channel, and a useful Facebook presence.

If you are worried about legal ramifications of engagement and consumer feedback, you can listen and monitor, blog with limited comments, create a podcast, or provide content that others can distribute and post to create awareness for your company. These are legitimate ways to take advantage of the technology without rocking the system too much.

The biggest gain of all?

The biggest potential benefit of social media technologies for many companies may have nothing to do with connecting with customers or creating great content for the public. It might be the opportunity to unleash the productivity of your own employees.

Your employees already enjoy using fun applications like social networks, blogs, and wikis. What if you applied this enthusiasm to the internal company environment?

The speed and scale of adopting social technologies by consumers is unprecedented, yet companies are far from capturing the impact of these platforms. Almost any human interaction that can be conducted electronically can be made "social," but only 5 percent of all potential uses now take place through social networks.

A report from the McKinsey Global Institute identified 10 ways in which social technologies can create savings across the value chain. They estimated that between $900 billion and $1.3 trillion in value can be unlocked in the U.S. alone from:

- Social networks

- Blogs and micro-blogs

- Ratings and reviews

- Social commerce

- Wikis

- Discussion forums

- Co-created content

- Crowd-sourcing

- Media and file sharing

- Social gaming

Spanning across all these categories is social analytics to enable better-informed decisions.

Two-thirds of the projected value comes from improving communications and collaboration across the enterprise. It gets at this idea of organizing a company around problem-solving instead of silos.

For example, in a large company, the expert company employee to solve a problem in the U.S. might actually be based in Australia. Social platforms can make employees aware of these problems and help unleash their skills through technology. McKinsey estimates implementing internal social systems could raise the productivity of knowledge workers by at least 20 percent. What a revolutionary opportunity!

Is your company a candidate for this type of social media application? Here's a profile of an ideal company:

- A high percentage of knowledge workers

- Heavy reliance on brand recognition or consumer perception

- A need to maintain a strong reputation to build credibility and consumer trust

- A digital distribution method for products or services

- An experiential (hotels) or inspirational product or service (sports products)

- Particularly fit for the social overhaul are consumer goods companies, education, professional services, media, and software companies, which have a high number of knowledge workers and a high reliance on brand recognition.

An example: Employees of the Dutch government are using web-based tools to share offices, conference spaces, and other resources. The employees were facing too many bureaucratic hurdles, and even had to reserve meeting space in their own buildings through an outside agency! One particularly frustrated employee tweeted her exasperation to colleagues, and they decided to form a group to build their own reservation system with open-source software. They rolled it out building by building, and now the system includes more than 53 offices and 554 work spaces across the country.

Essilor International, a global maker of ophthalmic lenses, created an internal training program that mixes in-person and Web 2.0 formats to transmit best practices among 102 sites in 40 countries. The company says that a mastery level that once took three years to achieve can now be reached in about one.

Rite-Solutions, a software company, built an internal idea marketplace that has so far generated 15 new commercial products that account for 20 percent of the company's total revenue. This system goes far beyond a typical brain-storming platform. The internal website connects potential new products with the resources, experience, and expertise that can bring ideas to life. The internal social networking site enables communities to organically develop to further improve, develop, and commercialize new product ideas.

The Mexico-based cement giant Cemex introduced an internal-collaboration platform called Shift, which has helped the company reduce the time needed to introduce new products and make internal process improvements. Shift uses a mix of wikis, blogs, discussion boards, and Web-conferencing tools to speed problem-solving. The payoff is lower cycle times, faster time to market, and real-time process improvement.

Five reasons to have a social media presence, even if you are still on the fence

---

Let's say you've given this book a thorough read, you've evaluated your strategy and your marketplace dispassionately, and, with strong reasoning and data, you've decided that you don't need any part of this social media scene. You can serve your customers, stave off competitors, and remain vital, profitable, and relevant without it. I suppose that might be possible in a few cases.

Well ... I'm not done with you yet. Here are five reasons you should STILL consider establishing a presence on the social web, even if you don't see a need for it today.

1. Search

There is a high-stakes war going on between Google and a

multi-billion-dollar industry called SEO (search engine optimization). The SEO's are trying to out-trick Google to make them think their customer's websites belong at the top of the search results. Google surreptitiously changes their algorithms to fight back. Then, the SEO's figure that out and create counter-measures ... and the war rages on and on.

One of the most important and significant changes the search engines have made to deliver meaningful and personal results is to incorporate social media activity as part of the validation process for content. It's too complicated to get into in this short book, but suffice to say that search engines are moving toward "warmer" search results based on known social media connections and recommendations.

Nearly every change Google has made in the past five years helps establish helpful, original content as a key driver in search rankings. Establishing authority on the web through your social media content could dramatically help you improve your organization's search rankings over time. And almost every business can benefit from that.

2. Facebook is the Internet

A common question I receive in my classes and workshops is, "What will be the next Facebook?" A point I try to make is that the emotional switching cost to moving away from Facebook is enormously high. That's where you have all your friends, photos, videos, and family members. It's where you have your Farmville farm for goodness sake!

I've made the argument that it might be easier to change your house than to change your social network.

Research from The Social Habit, a division of Edison Research, reveals that more than 80 percent of Americans between the ages of 13 and 24 are on Facebook and more than half are active every day. There is no other brand in the world that boasts that kind of market penetration. To this demographic, who either are, or soon will be, your customers, Facebook IS the Internet.

And the popular social network is rapidly spreading across every demographic and every region of the world. It is the largest media entity in the history of the world.

One interesting and significant trend is that the amount of search on Facebook has been rising dramatically. Since people are spending so much of their time there any way, they are also using Facebook like they used to use Google. Increasingly, Facebook will be the way people find and connect with goods, services, companies, and brands. It probably makes sense to stake your claim there, right? Who knows where the future will lead us?

3. Social proof

There is a particularly funny scene in the Will Ferrell movie *Elf* when he passes a run-down looking coffee shop that has a sign saying "World's Best Cup of Coffee." With exuberant joy, he bursts into the shop and yells "Congratulations!"

It's a hilarious moment, but a common example of "social proof" that has been used in the advertising world for decades. When we don't know the truth, we look for clues from our external environment (like a claim in a storefront window) to help us make decisions.

Social proof is not always true or accurate, it just has to provide an effective impression of authority.

In my book *Return On Influence*, I point to a famous example of this, actor Robert Young.

Young was an accomplished radio, film, and television actor who represented the iconic All-American father in the 1950s TV series "Father Knows Best." In the 1970s he reprised this squeaky-clean image in an even more famous character — the gentle, and trusted "Marcus Welby, M.D." In fact he became so tied to this character that it was impossible NOT to think of him in this role in any subsequent role or appearance he earned.

Despite his trademark portrayal of these happy, well-adjusted characters, Robert Young's reality could not have been more different. He admitted to being a terrible father and husband, and was often described as a bitter man. He suffered from depression and alcoholism, and spoke openly about a suicide attempt in the early 1990s.

Yet during this same time frame, Young was among America's most popular television commercial spokespersons – utterly in contrast to his tormented personal reality.

Brands capitalized on his social proof as a TV doctor and extended all of those powerful, positive attributes to their products, even though the man wrapped in the white lab coat was suffering as a human being.

In the online world, "social proof" is paramount ... and easily achieved because anybody can appear to be pumped-up and important, even when they're not.

There has never been a time in history where the mantle of authority has been so effortlessly assumed and promoted. Words like "best-selling," "award-winning" and "expert" have become meaningless.

And yet in our information-dense world of the Internet, we're starved for clues to help us determine leadership and authority and we readily turn to "badges of influence" like number of Twitter followers or Facebook Likes as convenient indicators of power.

Perhaps the most prestigious symbol of social proof today is the Facebook "Like." Among many companies, there is a Facebook arms race in progress as competing brands do anything necessary to gain the upper hand on this seemingly important metric. One large American consumer product company has an internal marketing metric of "cost per like." On the surface, this seems ludicrous but it demonstrates how strategically important this symbol has become.

This might seem a little "icky," but it's real. Don't overlook social proof of authority as a legitimate reason to have an active social media presence.

4. The Trade Show Dilemma

Have you ever had to sit at a booth during a large industry trade show?

I did, and I hated every minute of it. It was nice to network with people in the industry and maybe even chat with customers, but it was certainly not a very effective use of my time! Despite spending tens of thousands of dollars on this marketing event, we rarely sold anything, learned anything, or created any new value beyond handing out nice pens.

So why did we do it?

Because if we weren't there, people would think something was wrong. We would be ostentatiously absent.

"Wonder why Ajax Printing didn't come this year? Must be having financial problems."

"I wonder if Ajax is not at the trade show because they are pulling out of the industry?"

"Ajax isn't attending the show this year. As their largest competitor we can use that to our advantage!"

In this day and age, not being on Facebook or Twitter sends the same message. "Ajax Printing isn't on Facebook? I guess they just don't get it." Even if you DO get it, it tells a story that you don't get it. Having those social sharing buttons on your website is the new trade show. You better be there, even if it may not be the best use of your time.

5. Social media is the future of communications

Several large universities have stopped communicating with their students via email. Instead, they've set up Facebook Groups to handle class discussions and assignments.

The Net Generation – your next pool of employees, customers, and competitors – prefer to use the social web over any other form of communication. It is the natural evolution of communications. You might enjoy reading a paper copy of *The Wall Street Journal* each morning, or even looking at an online version of your favorite news site. Nearly half of Americans under the age of 21 cites Facebook as their primary source of news.

The social web is where a generation is going to connect, learn, and discover. Ignore this at your peril!

I know this was a long and complex chapter so let's review the basic concepts. Do you really need to have a social media strategy?

- Social media may be the only way your company is going to remain relevant in a digital age.

- Accurately defining your business strategy and being able to answer "Only we ..." is a critical first step to determine the extent of your presence on the social web.

- There are many applications of social media beyond just marketing. Think about how it might work for PR, HR, cost-savings, connecting with influencers, enhancing customer service, internal process improvements, reputation man-agement, and even as a source of ideas for new products and services.

- While there are legitimate considerations in regulated industries, there are still many opportunities to apply social media.

- The biggest opportunities might be in applying social tech-nologies to internal company processes.

- Finally, we discussed five strategic reasons to embark on a social media journey, even if it may not be in your current marketing plans.

By now you may be convinced that there is something to this social media stuff after all. So how much is it going to cost?

Questions leaders need to consider

1. Let's start at the top. Do we have a business strategy? Can we answer our "only we?"

2. Are we sure what our customers and competitors are doing in the social media space? If we haven't evaluated this in the last six months, let's look again.

3. Is there an opportunity to differentiate ourselves through a social media presence?

Chapter Eight

How much should we spend on social media marketing?

It's always frustrating trying to answer a question like this because of course there is no cookie-cutter answer. In fact, the answer to almost every marketing question like this is "it depends!"

A marketing strategy — and the appropriate budget — is going to be determined by your organization's goals and the competitive structure of your industry. Hopefully some of the ideas already presented in this book have you thinking about opportunities to apply these technologies in appropriate ways that can support your objectives.

To answer this question about budgeting, you need to dig deeply into the soul of your business and spend time answering questions such as:

■ Is our current marketing program and the traditional channels still working? Are they projected to be working a year from now?

■ Where are our customers getting their information today? How is this changing?

■ How are the demographics of our business shifting?

- Are our competitors using social media? If yes, how? If no, is that an opportunity to create a point of differentiation?

- What percent of our budget can we use to begin experimenting in this area?

- Do we have a source of rich content or some human resources that we can divert into a social media effort or do we need to look for other options?

- What is the risk of putting this off and falling behind? What is the advantage to creating a core competency in this area?

To optimize the opportunities behind a social media effort (no matter the size or complexity of the effort), I do believe organizations need to commit to budgeting in a consistent and patient way. Here's a traditional view of funding an advertising or promotional program:

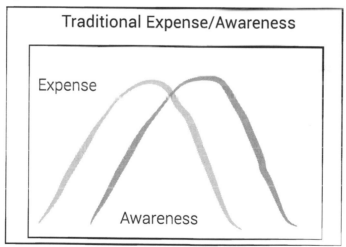

Of course this is a very simplified view, but in a traditional media spend, you might run an ad campaign and, after some lag, awareness increases and then abruptly drops when the ad campaign spending is over. This could be repeated over and over again and the persisting level of awareness would eventually increase because of the long-term commitment to advertising.

When approaching social media or content marketing, the commitment should be for the long haul. It's unlikely that you're going to strike lightning with your first few blog posts or Facebook updates. The idea is to drive relationships through consistent small engagements that eventually lead to awareness and bigger interactions, like a sale.

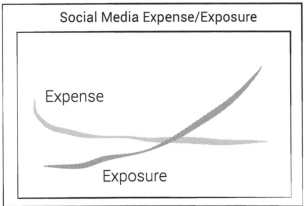

The idea behind this graph (again, very simplified) is that there is a start-up cost to build a social media competency but that it should become more efficient over time. Your costs will be level or perhaps even go down as you get into a groove.

At the same time, there is no immediate affect on awareness like you might get with an aggressive advertising campaign. Unless you are already a well-established brand, it takes time to build an audience that trusts you and looks to you for meaningful content and engagement.

It's likely that your company will invest in both paid and earned media and that the two will be integrated in some way. In that case, the expense of the integration and the effect on awareness would be blended:

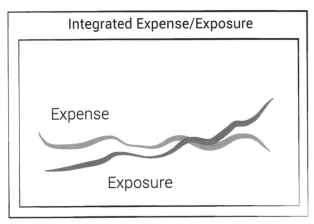

So that is a basic framework to consider if you're in the middle of your annual budgeting process. Again, there is no one-size-fits-all strategy or budget that you can apply uniformly across every company but I hope some of these fundamental ideas will help point you in the right direction.

How do we find the time to do this?

This is not a question. For many companies, it is THE question! The time, human resources, and talents needed to consistently populate the social web may seem overwhelming.

Let me give you an example of how using social media can actually SAVE you time.

When I started my own business, networking meetings seemed like the only option to build my business. Chamber of Commerce meetings. Networking "speed dating." Trade shows. Business Networking International.

I loathed this. And it took So. Much. Time.

Getting ready. Driving to the meeting. Shaking hands with people who were trying to sell me pest extermination services and carpet cleaning. Cold chicken sandwiches. Boring speakers. Driving back to the office. Sound familiar?

Sure, I met lots of nice people, but they were all trying to sell something to ME, too. I acquired a few small local customers but they were unprepared to think and work on the strategic level I enjoyed. They needed yard signs, not company strategies. If I stuck with it, I could have made a living, but I needed to paint on a much bigger canvas.

Luckily for me, this era of my life coincided with the dawn of Twitter. I hated it at first. The first tweet I ever received was "it's 4 a.m." confirming that indeed, this really was the stupidest thing mankind had ever dreamed up.

But to be a consultant and teacher, I had to stick with it and try to understand what all the buzz was about. Twitter is deceptively simple, but it took me 4-6 months to understand it ... and I continue to learn every day.

The social media networking revolution

I enjoyed the fascinating people, humor, and intelligence that surrounded me once I got in the Twitter groove. And I didn't realize it at the time, but I had stumbled upon the greatest business networking opportunity in the history of the world.

I was connecting with extraordinary people who would have been impossible to know just a few years earlier. Many connections became friendships. The friendships went offline into phone calls and meetings. The synergies seemed to multiply day by day and soon I was collaborating on projects, hiring Twitter connections for freelance work, and helping others find employment.

And best of all, I could do it from the comfort of my own home without those endless cold chicken sandwiches and 45-minute drives to the meeting site. And ... it was FUN.

As the enormous benefits of Twitter networking accumulated, I stopped the time-consuming and expensive local meetings completely. Today, I have a thriving international business built almost entirely through social networking. My three largest customers, five most important collaborators, and my teaching position at Rutgers University all came to me via connections I made through social media.

A lot of people get overwhelmed by the amount of time you can devote to social networking. Well, have you ever compared this to the time involved in REAL LIFE networking? In just the amount of time I was spending in my car, I could write blog posts for a week or devote enough time to network on Twitter for a month!

To embark on this social media journey, you're going to have to make some changes in the way you do business. That is never an easy thing to consider. But maybe it's time to make a few adjustments.

Re-thinking your business

I have a customer who is spending $70,000 per month on full-page newspaper advertising. Recently the CMO told me that she had a feeling that they just aren't working like they used to. Gee ... do you think so?

Another large engineering company is still producing a glossy company magazine every month. Why? So people can throw it out? If you put it on the web, the content lives forever. The marketing leadership of that company is afraid to force their people to change, afraid to rock the boat, afraid to upset a traditional publication. I smell "Rand" in the air.

Blow up your marketing budget and examine where you *really need to be.* It's not fair to your employees to simply pile on more work. What needs to go away? If you took just 25 percent of that $70,000 monthly newspaper marketing budget and devoted it to social media marketing, you could have a pretty substantial start.

The resource imperative

If there is one common budgeting consideration for any effort, for any company, in any industry, it would be this: Spend the money (especially upfront) to get the expert guidance and the appropriate resources you need to be successful.

Small or medium companies might choose to out-source this expertise, at least for a period of time, until a decision can be made about creating an internal core competency in this area. Moving to a social media marketing strategy is a big change and a big challenge. It's unlikely that you will have the necessary resources in-house. It is certainly appropriate to get some outside help to get you rapidly up the learning curve and in the end it will probably save you money.

Larger companies will almost certainly want an in-house community manager to coordinate the content and engagement strategy. Over time, you may also need resources dedicated to listening/monitoring, content creation, customer service, reporting, and other functions, but at a minimum, every company needs somebody to own the role of community manager.

The best community managers are like a good event planner or party host. A party host will connect people, welcome incoming guests appropriately, maintain conversations throughout the event, and see everyone safely off with a smile and a wave. They will pay attention to the ambiance of the meeting space, and get to know individual needs. If something goes wrong, they know how to handle the situation with grace.

Communications is also an essential community manager skill, and that includes an ability to listen. Personality is going to come through so that is an important consideration as you establish your company's online "voice."

Community managers are both ambassadors and advocates. This is complex, but a community manager's first responsibility is to their employer, and yet, he or she must convey the voice of the people (customers and other stakeholders) so the company fully understands the mood of the marketplace, the needs of the people, and the customer's intentions. Further, the community manager must clearly understand the community's position in the marketplace and communicate that in such a way that customers don't feel they are being fed a press release.

Finally, community managers have the responsibility to populate the metrics and create the reports needed to translate the efforts into value. The best resources know enough about your business and management style to continually adjust to the subtle needs of the business. Don't overlook the need for this person to have strong analytical skills.

I also suggest that your company create a Social Media Lead Team consisting of the managers most directly involved in the effort, the community manager, and perhaps a representative from PR, IT, and Legal.

The purpose of the Social Media Lead Team is to ensure that the necessary support and resources are available and deployed to activate this cultural change. In this start-up phase, the team should probably meet at least once a month for two hours, with the amount of time and frequency diminishing as the changes take hold. The Lead Team will:

- Review monthly metric dashboard

- Solve resource issues

- Provide positive reinforcement and recognition to those embracing change

- Actively demonstrate their leadership and interest in digital business through their work on this team

- Review and enforce the company social media policy

- Decide on the timing of significant new projects

The Lead Team also provides continuity should the community manager leave the company.

Take it one step at a time

I'd like to conclude this chapter with a story from a young man who was facing what you might be facing right now -- Starting a social media effort from scratch with limited budget and experience.

Bill Piper was one of my students and eventually went on to do some pretty big things around social media and marketing. I like his slow and steady approach. Here's his story:

Several months ago, I was handed the reins to my company's digital brand.

I didn't know what I was doing. At all.

I'm a young marketer and enjoy social media for myself, but the most I knew about digital B2B marketing was that I could really blow it. I work for a cutting-edge IT company, so our ambition was to do social media in the same manner: on the cutting-edge, and with excellence.

Starting from square one, I knew that I needed a solid plan with executable tasks and guidance from someone who had been where I wanted to go. So I took Mark's social media marketing class and learned a sustainable process to drive our desired business benefits (revenue) over the long haul.

We started implementing our strategy earlier this year with blogging, SEO, and a few social media outlets. We haven't done it perfectly. It hasn't been impressive. But the thing is – it has WORKED!

We've secured sales leads, generated revenue, and solidified our brand recognition through social media.
I'm not an expert but I've outlined a set of principles that have worked, even when I had to work above my experience level.

Make humility work for you – For most of us, an honest and objective look at ourselves should enable an attitude of humility. The difficult part is that it's not always easy. To be successful, figure out the people smarter and better at their jobs than you are and ask them lots of questions. Who is the "Mark Schaefer" in your community? There are lots of gurus out there but who can work with you but who really knows what he or she is doing? We all want to look smart, but asking for help and assuming a humble attitude of learning can be your biggest asset in developing your skill sets.

Focus. Develop your skills one by one – Given the breadth of digital strategies, there's a lot of knowledge and savvy that goes into successful marketing. What are the top three marketing skill sets you need to develop? Pick one at a time, get really good at it and move on to the next. For me, it made sense to become proficient in some search engine optimization skills first, then blogging, and then Twitter, etc. and, I'm going to keep learning, too.

Be committed and decisive – With inexperience and uncertainty it's easy to over-think things. When faced with uncertainty, I found it important to make the best decision I could at that specific time. I acknowledged that I didn't know all the variables at play but would move forward expecting to make adjustments. I couldn't commit to being perfect, but I could commit to constant forward motion.

You don't have to be perfect in your social media execution. We're all still learning, and there are probably things I should be doing that I haven't even heard about yet. At the end of the day, though, I'm content with my ignorance-expert status as long as we *keep getting results.*

The lesson I take from Bill is focus, start small, ask for help, and keep learning. For most businesses, this is a very smart approach to budgeting, gaining traction and finding your way steadily and surely in the big world of digital marketing.

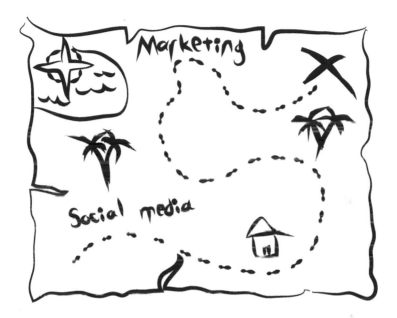

Questions leaders need to consider

1. Is it time to re-examine how we are spending our marketing dollars? How has our effectiveness changed?

2. What part of our budget could we afford to commit NOW to social media marketing?

3. If we needed to focus and excel in just one area, what should that be?

Chapter Nine

What do we do about these negative comments?

One of the most common social media fears I hear from business leaders is the risk of opening their company up to public criticism ... or worse. Of course this is a natural concern and a real issue in a world where everyone can publish and rant. Let's take a look at this issue and make some rational sense of it.

A few years ago, I was in charge of re-inventing a customer service department for a large company. During the process I searched for all the help I could get from published reports on best practices. The most important paper I found came from the University of Michigan Business School. A team of academics had studied the cost versus benefit of trying to achieve "100 percent customer satisfaction."

The study came to two very important conclusions.

1) The cost of satisfying dissatisfied customers is typically very low. Most people simply want to be acknowledged and assured that the problem is being addressed. Just good, normal business, right?

2) The other conclusion was that less than 2 percent of your dissatisfied customers are probably "haters" who will never be satisfied no matter what you do. They will try to "game you" for more goodies, harass you no matter how you respond, and just be

an annoying pain for any company because that is how they get attention.

Their conclusion was that in most cases, it is economically unwise to try to shoot for 100 percent customer satisfaction because an inordinate amount of your resources will be tied up in that angry 2 percent. The implication is -- forget about them. Go ahead and lose those customers because they are too expensive to maintain.

Unfortunately that advice takes on new meaning in an era where every person can publish, post, and tweet. That 2 percent may very well control the conversation. They don't just go away. They get worse.

Is your house in order?

If you have reliable products and good customer service, you're probably not going to be getting a lot of people hating you. A study I completed for a large company in the hospitality industry showed that .02 percent of the Facebook comments in their industry were negative – that is two hundredths of a percent. Hardly anything to lose sleep over and that is fairly typical if you have your house in order.

But what if you DON'T have your house in order?

One of the themes in this book is the importance of establishing an organizational culture that can support the openness and responsiveness required by the social web. That is not always easy.

The social media policy

A key ingredient of getting your house in order is establishing a social media policy for your company. This is an essential guide to help establish boundaries and expectations as your employees try to find their way on the social web.

Regardless of the size of your company, you need a social media policy to protect your company and your employees. Chances are, you already have employee policies about safety, sick days, and appropriate technology use. You also need to have a policy about how your company communicates with the outside world.

In my city, a teacher was recently suspended from her job for posting information about a student on a Facebook page. It was not her page, the school district's page, or even the student's page. She was on her own time and using a personal computer. Still, she was held responsible for her personal behavior and the school district was embarrassed because they had no social media policy they could point to justifying their action.

A few key elements that should be included in your social media policy:

- Who can participate for the company? When? Where?

- Legal considerations

- Who owns the accounts?

- Who owns the content?

- What can employees do from home?

- Expectations of online conduct

- Accountabilities and responsibilities

- Examples of what would be considered abuse in terms of time spent on the social web

■ Policies to follow if an emergency occurs like a social-media-generated threat

Plenty has been written about this subject and there are many, many resources on the web to help guide you. In fact at http://socialmediagovernance.com/policies.php you can find hundreds of examples of social media policies. Your policy needs to be integrated into your employee training and culture and reviewed for relevancy every six months.

Insulating yourself from negativity

A social media policy can help guide employees but it can do nothing to insulate you if you have chronic customer service issues. This is an important step – you must expose and address those issues before they become a public embarrassment. Here's an example ...

I worked with a company that was literally paralyzed by fear over the possibility of negative comments. They were so fearful in fact that their competitors were zooming by them and their investors were becoming alarmed. They brought me in to help figure out a strategy.

I spent the first day just listening and learning in their customer service department. This was the heart of the company and I needed to discover how the customers connected to them, what was on their minds, and the potential opportunities for solving customer problems through a social media strategy.

What I found shocked me.

The service center was highly efficient and skilled at handling customer inquiries until there was a really serious problem. If a complaint was escalated to a supervisor, the customer waited on hold for an average of 10 minutes and it was not unusual for people to wait 30 minutes or more ... if they did not abandon the call. To quantify the problem, we started collecting data for a few months and this verified that the company's current method of dealing with problems was actually creating thousands of potential social media haters every month.

This is a great company. A well-managed company. But they were stuck in an antiquated system that had not kept up with the changing marketplace. Perhaps before the days of the social web a company could get away with this in the short-term, but in this era, every angry customer waiting on hold is a potential social media terrorist.

What do you think they are going to be doing while they are waiting all that time? Complaining on Facebook! Whacking you on Twitter!

My advice was for this company to do nothing about starting their Facebook page until they could address this serious customer service issue, which they did.

Another customer of mine introduced a new product and it became an unexpected sensation. This was a good problem to have but the company had to aggressively add capacity and work like mad to keep the shipments going. They were proud that under the circumstances of overwhelming growth, they had achieved a 98 percent on-time shipping performance.

Sounds impressive, right? But in the social media era, is that good enough?

The company was shipping 2 million units per month. If 2 percent of the shipments were late, that means 40,000 people were unhappy. According to the university study I referred to, about 2 percent of those people could be "haters" who receive some psychological benefit from making a company miserable. That means they were creating 800 new haters every month.

You would expect that a lot of these haters would start venting about their late shipments on Facebook and Twitter.

And that is exactly what happened.

They complained and complained and complained. It was ugly. The company became so overwhelmed by social media complaints that their customer service department could not keep up, which made it even worse. Within a few weeks, the Facebook page had become toxic. Their employees were overwhelmed. My advice? Shut the Facebook page down and right the ship by solving the shipment problem and creating a customer service department that could handle the expectations of the social media age. That is the reality of our world. Deal with it. Adjust. Adapt.

Now I don't mean to scare you off. But I do want to make a strong point: Get your house in order because the social web will make you miserable if you don't.

Remember foundation number one

Even if you have your house in order, sometimes bad stuff happens in business.

Today, even something that starts small can wreak havoc if it's not handled appropriately.

For the vast majority of companies, complaints are an opportunity to show what they are made of. It's basic good business – acknowledge the complaint has been heard, apologize, and respond in a prompt and courteous way.

Over time, you may even view complaints as gifts. If you're screwing up, why wouldn't you want to know and fix it? These folks are bringing their problem to your turf instead of spreading toxicity throughout their communities. Isn't that a GOOD thing?

If you commit to a helpful and human social media presence over the long term, people will notice and actually come to your defense if the haters show up. I recently witnessed this when a famous restaurant received some terrible publicity about an awful health inspection report. One hater came on to their Facebook page and not only delivered some pretty negative comments, he would not let go.

The restaurant responded quickly and compassionately. They explained the situation and stated their plan to correct it. When the hater kept whining, other fans of the restaurant came to their defense, saying "They explained the problem and are correcting it. What more do you want?" The community shut down the "hater" and the restaurant didn't have to do another thing.

The key challenge for a business is listening and responding in a rapid fashion. Research from The Social Habit (sponsored by Edison Research) showed that about half of those surveyed (Americans) said they expected a resolution to an online complaint in 60 minutes or less! Are you ready for that?

The big brands are gearing up for that service level and that sets the expectations for everyone. Turning a negative into a positive is an opportunity -- but not responding quickly, effectively, and humanly can make things worse.

I should mention that a number of research reports support the idea that SOME negative reviews are actually helpful and may even increase sales because it validates the credibility of the claims. Another way to look at it!

A culture of commitment

It is a truly exceptional organization that is NEVER going to get negative comments, so preparing for them before they happen is an essential part of this cultural transition. Is your management team ready for negative comments? Here is a possible response plan for your company to consider and adopt.

1. Make a commitment to respond to all complaints with honesty. It doesn't have to be a full-blown response approved by the legal department, but it has to be a timely acknowledgment that the complainer has been heard. Remember, that takes care of 98 percent of the problems!

2. Acknowledge their right to complain. Show some empathy and try to defuse the emotion by saying something like "Yes, I'd be upset if that happened to me."

3. Apologize if warranted. And, maybe even if it isn't warranted.

4. Empower employees to solve the issue on the spot if it is some

thing simple, or have the respondent offer to take the issue offline through a phone call or email.

5. Follow up. Assess specifically what is needed to make the person feel better. If you drop the ball in this phase, expect the emotion and response to escalate.

6. If the problem persists even after if you have offered a reasonable remedy, either escalate to skilled internal resources or abdicate based on the risk and legitimate severity of the problem.

Let's look at what happens when a company does not follow this simple plan – and I was the case study!

A Fortune 100 company, Verizon, apparently used content from my blog and posted it on their own website as if it were their original content. There was no reference that the content came from my blog and didn't even list an author or provide a link. They had never asked for permission to use my content for their own commercial purposes.

To make matters worse, I had actually paid a writer to develop this original content, so they were benefiting not only from my work, but from my budget! Their practice was not only bad business, it was illegal because it violated copyright law.

I figured it was some sort of mistake and because I'm genuinely interested in this sort of thing, I decided to send in an inquiry to figure out how it had happened. Like most complainers, I just wanted an explanation and an apology.

I emailed customer service twice. I called them twice. I left messages for them on Twitter and Facebook, simply asking for a response. I wrote their VP of corporate communications twice and finally called him. I heard nothing from the company.

After 10 weeks, I finally got a return call from somebody in the communication department. She was kind, apologetic, and told me she would call me the next day with an explanation. I never heard from her again.

Finally, as a pure coincidence, I had a student in one of my college classes from the company's customer service department.

I explained the problem to her and in a few days the woman who actually ran the website that used my content called me.

Her response was a disaster. She was rude and defensive. She had not bothered to look seriously at the problem and in fact, blamed it on another company they had hired to "scrape" content from the web to populate their website – a lazy and problematic way to fill a content hole. She appeared to just want to get me off the phone and ended by saying that the company who scraped the content would send me a gift certificate to cover the costs of what I paid my author.

This three-month episode was so aggravating and had wasted so much of my time – despite my goodwill -- that I had reached a tipping point. I decided to do something I had never done before – I wrote a blog post about this company and the incident. The post went viral, attracting more than 1,000 shares on the social web and over 100 comments, all blistering this company. One of my readers was so appalled by this account she vowed to never do business with this company.

I then received a call from Ragan Communications, wanting to re-publish that article in their newsletter (the leading daily communication to PR professionals) ... with proper attribution and links of course! This attracted hundreds of additional shares and comments directed at the company. Other bloggers blogged about my blog (that makes sense right?) further spreading the story to untold thousands of additional readers.

Once the issue went viral, I was contacted by a representative of Verizon's PR department who promised to "fix this." She requested more information and although I was in the middle of an overseas business trip, I sent her a lengthy email explaining the issue – the eighth time I had sent this information to Verizon. I never received a response from her.

This is an example of a company that did not have their house in order and the situation eventually spun out of control. Let's look at this case study in the context of my guidelines for handling complaints.

First, paying a company to blindly scrape content from the web is never a good idea. This is different than categorizing and adding new insight and value through legitimately curating content. Their house was not in order. This was a disaster waiting to happen.

In addition, their customer service department was not equipped to handle a non-technical consumer complaint. They "wrote up a ticket" which became lost in their system. So their legacy service capabilities could not handle new input from the web. Also, the company has so many different Twitter and Facebook accounts, it is hard to figure out where to go to get attention to a problem. These are more examples of not having the house in order to begin with, which exacerbated what began as a small problem.

Week after week, month after month, my patient inquiries were ignored. When I finally got a call, the person was defensive and rude. She did not acknowledge my right to complain. This effectively turned me from a curious customer into an aggravated blogger.

Despite promises of a resolution from PR, customer service, corporate communications, and, finally, the person behind the website, there was no follow-up. This ended up being the final straw which made me take my case public (remember that lesson from early in the book about immediacy?).

We can see that this is a company that is ill-prepared for life on the web. They are not making the cultural transition needed to thrive in this new environment.

If the company had just responded in 24 hours with a simple explanation and an apology, they would have maintained me as a happy and loyal customer.

Business life on the web is more complex, but it can also be an opportunity to create a point of differentiation and undying customer loyalty if you get it right!

Questions leaders need to consider

1. As we have seen, so much of social media success is determined by the culture of the company. Is your company ready to make a commitment to answer all complaints?

2. How do we get started with a social media policy? Are there pre-existing examples that can guide us?

3. Is our house in order? Have we buffered ourselves from criticism as much as possible?

Chapter Ten

We have limited resources. Where do we start?

If your company made ladders and sold them to big chain stores, how much of your budget should you spend on social media marketing?

Should you step it up? (Sorry, I can't help myself sometimes). Where would you even begin to determine a strategy specific to your market opportunities? Where do you start? How do you prioritize my resources?

These are more than academic questions. These are the essential issues many companies are struggling with today.

As we have already established, most companies should have a social media presence today. So let's assume you're like 95 percent of the businesses out there: You need to do it. You want to do it. You don't know where to start.

When I'm working with new clients, the roadmap basically boils down to following the line behind five essential questions. These are not easy questions, but if you really work through them, your social media plan will become self-evident. You'll know where to start, and you'll be able to identify the resources needed to succeed.

KEY QUESTION NUMBER 1: Can you finish this sentence? "Only we ..."

Of course we covered this angle in Chapter 7 but this is

where you need to start your journey and I can't over-emphasize its importance.

Working this question forces you to figure out why you're distinctive, why your customers love you, and how you fit in your marketplace. Strategy is about finding something that is different, valuable, and hopefully sustainable, about your organization.

And by the way, your "only we" will probably shift over time. I think it is rare today that a business can count on a "long term" advantage. It's more about occupying a certain place in time and space, and adjusting with that space as the market, technology, and competitors change.

My favorite example of this ideal is Coca-Cola. What is their competitive advantage? The product is only colored sugar water, right? Yet, they continually re-invent themselves to stay relevant in the minds of their consumers, generation after generation.

Here's an effective intervention I use when a customer seems to be hazy about their strategy. I gather the top executives around a table and have them get out a piece of paper. Then I ask each of them to answer the "only we ... " question in writing.

In any company I have worked with -- big or small, high-tech or a commodity business -- there has never been concordance in the answers. This is always a revelation, and perhaps a small embarrassment to the leaders. But it sparks the right discussion -- if we can't articulate our essential place in the market to ourselves, are we really all rowing in the right direction? What IS it that we really do?

Often, the first suggested "only we" is something like "we create exceptional value for our customers through our integrity and quality products." No. I don't think so. That's something that nearly every company in the world wants to claim, right? What is it that is exceptional about YOU? And ONLY you?

If you want the right answer, usually the best place to start is your customers.

Talk to them. Survey them. Even better, go pay them a visit.

What do they think sets you apart and why? Why do they love you? Why do they keep coming back?

What is keeping them up at night? What does the future hold? What are their un-met and under-served needs? How do we fit in this puzzle?

Without exception, when I do this customer work, a common theme eventually emerges, and often it is something we didn't expect at all -- sometimes what a company is selling is not necessarily what the customer is buying!

Here's an example of what I mean. I once had a customer who sold very complicated business communication systems. Their marketing was focused on being techy, techy, techy. Geeky, geeky, geeky.

But when I met with their customers and asked them why they bought from this company, we discovered that the customers could care less about the technology. In fact they didn't understand it ... and didn't want to. They loved this company because they were the authority in this field and could be trusted to look after their needs no matter what happened.

"I love this company," one customer told me. "Because we had an outage at 2 in the morning and by 2:30 the problem was fixed."

"I don't have to understand what they do," another said, "because no matter how the technology changes, I trust them to keep us up to date."

The company thought they were selling technology. But what the customer was buying was "peace of mind." We had found my client's "only we."

We completely revised their marketing message and social media strategy to reflect the idea that this company was "Your Business Communication Authority."

Customers almost always hold the keys to the marketing strategy kingdom!

KEY QUESTION NUMBER 2: Can our culture nurture and sustain a social media transformation?

The second issue to consider before you start is company culture. It doesn't matter how much money you have or how great your plan is ... culture will ALWAYS be your biggest enabler of success, or the biggest hurdle to your progress.

No matter where I go in the world, the same five corporate cultural hurdles come up over and over again:

- **Budget and resources** ("We already have a full plate. We don't have time for something new.")

- **ROI and measurement** ("Until you can demonstrate an ROI for Twitter, the project is on hold.")

- **IT – Tech support** (We're too busy figuring out cloud computing to help with your Facebook app.")

- **Legal and regulatory** ("The Legal Department will have to approve everything we publish each day.")

- **Culture and change management** ("I tried Twitter and I hated it. Nobody on the board uses it either so our company doesn't need it.")

Sound familiar?

If the company culture doesn't align with the requirements of being a "social organization," you will never create sustainable change.

As you create marketing plans for your own business — or if your current efforts are stagnating — maybe it's time to step back and look at how these five factors might be affecting your own social media success. Focusing on removing the internal roadblocks will give you the only chance of long-term marketing success.

KEY QUESTION NUMBER 3: Are we a conversational brand ... or could we be? At what cost and risk?

Here is the business case for Facebook in one sentence: "Come waste time with me."

Nobody HAS to be on Facebook. People pile on there every day to play Farmville or to see pictures of cats in dresses. Why in the world would they pay attention to you? If you work for Disney, Nike, or a movie studio, you have nothing to worry about. You have a beloved, conversational brand.

But if you're selling ladders? Maybe not so much ... unless you can MAKE yourself into a conversational brand. There are many famous examples of this, most notably the Blend-Tec "Will it Blend" video series. Yes, by blending marbles, iPads, and dozens of other improbable objects, they actually made blenders conversational. And you could probably do it with step ladders, too. But let's keep it real. That is not easy, and it's probably not cheap, so you have to weigh the risk and investment in creating extraordinary content with your other marketing options. If you're selling ladders, perhaps a coupon at the point of purchase would work better than investing in a video series. We need to keep marketing common sense in mind.

As I mentioned in Chapter 7, there are lots of solid business reasons to be on the social web even if you're not conversational ... research, marketing insight, customer service, and SEO to name a few. But sorting out this question ... Are we conversational, or can we be ... is probably going to be the biggest determinant of the budget you put into this effort. Becoming conversational is a huge opportunity, but it's not easy.

KEY QUESTIONS NUMBER 4: Where are our customers and competitors?

This seems like such a basic question but it is often overlooked. Doing just a little market research can be extraordinarily revealing.

I am working with an awesome new cancer treatment center. All of their competitors can brag about great equipment, compassionate doctors, and beautiful facilities. So how can my customer stand out?

A careful analysis of competitors showed that there was a wide open opportunity to create an effective social media presence. An analysis of customers shows that the web is by far the number one place people go to get their questions answered about cancer treatment options. They can actually use their social media marketing platform as a point of differentiation.

What about for the ladder company? How do customers

make decisions – do they conduct research ahead of time, search online, or make a purchase decision on the spot based on the lowest price in the store?

And what can we learn about our competitors? Do we have room to maneuver in this social media space or are there dominant players already?

Your industry structure and terms of competitive engagement always have a powerful impact on your marketing strategy. It makes sense to analyze this area carefully for potential leverage in the social media space.

KEY QUESTION NUMBER 5: What is our source of consistent, sustainable rich content?

Once you've been able to answer these first four questions, it's time to start thinking about the potential "fuel" for your social media effort.

Many companies are generating social media activity for the sake of activity. This is rarely a good idea. It means you're checking a box but probably not creating any real value.

If you're going to create new business benefits, solve problems, establish a leading voice of authority, and engineer opportunities for massive reach, you're going to have to do something more than tweet now and then or update your company's LinkedIn profile. You need to have a consistent source of "rich content" that becomes the engine of your social media presence.

As I discussed in Chapter 5, rich content is in-depth, searchable, quotable, and evergreen (meaning it can be relevant for months or years). Generally this means you need a blog, a podcast, or a video series, although Pinterest boards, Instagram accounts, eBooks, and other forms of presentations might do in some businesses.

The challenge is doing this on a consistent and sustainable basis. I've worked with a number of large and small companies to help them develop a culture of content creation and there seems to be a few common themes that enable success. Here are some steps that launch a company toward a vibrant culture of content creation:

1. Use the whole buffalo

The first question many companies ask is, "Where is all of this content going to come from?" They don't realize they may already be sitting on a wealth of resources.

When Native American Indians killed a buffalo for food they wasted nothing, using every part of the animal to make clothes, shelter, and weapons. Likewise, we should inventory all of our company content assets and leverage them to the max so that these existing investments are not wasted. Regular sources of superb content may already be coming to you through the form of:

- speeches

- customer presentations

- visits from guests and customers (why not do a video?)

- customer service bulletins

- investor communications

- marketing materials

- PR efforts

- employee newsletters

If I write one great blog post, there might be additional opportunities to turn this into an infographic, a presentation on SlideShare, posts on Facebook, Twitter and LinkedIn, and perhaps even an eBook. If I turn the presentation into a series of Power-Point slides, I could narrate that and put it on YouTube. All of this from one blog post.

Try to extract as much value from the content you have by tailoring it to the social web and igniting it across multiple channels. Use your whole buffalo!

2. Start with passionate volunteers

Starting an initiative to create original content can come as a shock to an organization. One idea for success is to start where you are going to have the best chance for success — passionate volunteers.

Author and consultant Jay Baer once said that, "if you don't love social media you will suck at social media" ... so find the people who already love it. In my mind this may be more important than finding people with writing ability or even marketing experience. Go to where the passion resides.

One company I work with started with five passionate volunteer bloggers and it grew to more than 200 in two years — organically! The enthusiasm spread from the passionate core.

3. Hire short-term help

It's not fair to "pile on" new content management duties when your people already have full time jobs. When just starting out, think about hiring an outside editor to help you get going. The duties would include:

- Assisting with the content plan and keeping it on track

- Assuring that content goes through the proper internal reviews

- Editing volunteer content and making sure it is appropriate and relevant

- Coaching company bloggers to help them improve

- Assure that blog comments and questions are being addressed

As your initiative grows, you will reach critical mass where you can consider hiring a full-time internal community manager to handle these tasks. Bring in an experienced resource to help give you your best chance for success.

4. Build-in quick wins

You need to "market your marketing" internally as well as externally. Reward bloggers and highlight their successes. One company maintains a leader board of bloggers who reach certain milestones and then rewards the top contributors with special events and company merchandise.

Build the opportunity for quick wins into your content marketing plan and promote with your internal leaders. Showing off the fun and success of your content team will get others interested in participating. Make it exciting. Build momentum.

5. Bring in some Top Guns

In addition to employee-created content, many companies also feature content from outside industry experts. Typically this is a paid assignment, but some authors are happy to do it for the exposure. This has a couple of strategic advantages:

- Adds instant credibility to your content marketing effort

- Provides third party validation to your company and brand

- Attracts fans of the author to your blog and to your company

- Can jump-start subscriptions and engagement

- Establishes a baseline of high quality "evergreen" content

Well, I hope this provides some useful ideas on how to start your social media program. Let's bring it home in one final chapter and see how this all works together in the real world.

Questions leaders need to consider

1. What is our "only we…" ?

2. What is our source of rich content?

3. How do we use the "whole buffalo?"

4. As a leader, what changes do I need to make to reinforce this culture of content creation?

Chapter Eleven

An awesome case study that pulls it all together

Does this stuff WORK?

Before I wrote this book, I made sure the ideas I've presented were battle-tested. I blogged about them, gave speeches about them, experimented with them, and taught them extensively to executives at a masters-level program at Rutgers University.

I honed the message and the delivery to a point where I knew it was getting through and making a real difference. I have seen the results over and over, and I know what I have provided in this book works.

One of my test beds for these principles was the B2B sales team at a Fortune 100 company (they have asked to not be mentioned by name). Over the years, I've worked on a number of projects for this company including an intensive set of training sessions for internal social media advocates from across the country.

And while most of the training attendees consumed the workshops from the comfort of their laptops some place, there was always this one guy, attending every live session, sitting in the front row, and asking all the questions. His name is Sander Biehn.

Clearly the idea of applying these principles to a large and complex organization had caught the attention of this man, and I cheered him on as he caught fire with a passion to integrate these concepts in the real world. Here is his story, in Sander's own words ...

I helped my company get $47 million in new business through a content-centered social media sales strategy.

Late in 2011, my company put together a new sales team to re-build business relationships with a huge and important company in Atlanta. We decided to take an entirely new approach that heavily favored building relationships through social media. We HAD to try something new. Our relationship with this client had suffered in the past five years, creating strain between our executive offices. All sales had dried up.

With training from Mark Schaefer and support from our internal team, we began implementing a content strategy aimed at strategic "persons of interest" from our former customer.

This created unique new opportunities to discuss and connect away from the heat of the emotion between our companies. Slowly, we saw a thaw and a major shift in the relationship started. This led to productive conversations about the business solutions that were being discussed in the targeted content.

Inside of 18 months, $47 million in brand new business was awarded to my company, directly attributable to our social media outreach.

Did that get your attention?

Good. Now let's cover how it actually worked — a successful social sales strategy.

The Social Sales Strategy

To make this work, we knew from the onset we would have to place exceptional content related to potential solutions in front of our customer. But what would that content be? To do this the sales team first looked at available solutions that were best suited to the customer's vertical market. There were a total of 10 solutions targeted. We needed to teach our customers about these unique opportunities in a helpful way.

We decided that the primary source of this new content would be our company blog.

Of course putting content out there was not enough. We also had to let them know it was out there and build an audience. Making sure the content was viewed by "persons of interest" at the client was the next part of the strategy. To do this, we settled on leveraging two social sites that our research told us customers most likely frequented: Twitter and LinkedIn. By placing original content in front of budget owners we reasoned that my company would be viewed as a thought-leader and we would not only be invited to bid, but we would be pre-disposed to win these RFP's.

Tactics

Content - One initial hurdle was finding exceptional content to place our technology in just the right light. The content that existed was targeted at technologists, not business people, and often had too much of a sales slant. Our new effort needed to be focused more on the customer's business and discuss their problems in their vernacular. We needed to be helpful.

To better align with this target group, we wrote entirely new posts customized to the customer and their roles. The content was not only approachable and business-focused, it was also personal to help us build relationships and encourage engagement with the authors. No ghost writing. We did the work.

Moving the Content —
As Mark Schaefer preaches, content is only powerful if it moves. We needed to build a relevant network.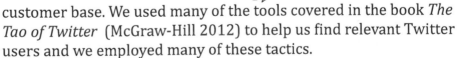

Our first place to go was Twitter, probably the fastest way to build a network. I first had to connect with Twitter users in our customer base. We used many of the tools covered in the book *The Tao of Twitter* (McGraw-Hill 2012) to help us find relevant Twitter users and we employed many of these tactics.

I looked to connect not only with customers who had job functions in areas where I believed there was budget for our solutions, but we also targeted industry specialists. Routine engagement with this targeted group included re-tweets and replies to tweets that they sent. Additionally, when there was positive press about the customer I made sure to tweet that and mention key contacts congratulating them on their work to get on their radar screen.

I also tweeted relevant articles from our blog and else-where. Finally, I tried to engage these customers with the customized content from the posts I wrote by not only tweeting it but also asking specific questions related to the content and mentioning the customers and people of interest from Twitter. I received engagement from the customers, who began to ask questions or agree or challenge points we made in the blog posts.

I approached LinkedIn in a similar fashion by using well-established methods to find people in our customer base who performed the functions most likely to hold budget for the solutions we were targeting. I then examined the LinkedIn Groups that these people belonged to and correlated the groups between customers to find the groups most likely to have the largest base of potential customers attached. Sometimes these were industry groups or groups associated with the job functions or even a group dedicated to employees of the customer.

The employee LinkedIn group for our customer had more than 5,000 members. After joining the groups I also began to interact there. I posed questions, tried to bring in helpful answers whenever possible, and posted relevant articles and ideas from the industry and even from our competitors. Of course I was sure to post positive news about our customer and mention group members by name if they were involved with the news items.

Occasionally I dropped in our targeted blog content, which also elicited engagement when we asked questions and solicited opinions and ideas.

Results

The reaction to our authentically helpful content and engagement was palpable. After several months of consistent engagement, I began getting questions — and then requests to bid for projects — that mirrored the information we were providing on our 10 strategic solutions.

This was an enormous breakthrough. Remember that relations between our companies had been icy and not exactly conducive to business. Our social media presence was changing the relationship with the customer.

We were being regarded as an expert resource and we were building relationships with people from new departments that had been out of contact with us. They told us our approach was "refreshing" because we were building relationships without bombarding them with phone calls, emails, and meetings (like the competition).

The ultimate proof of the power of social media marketing was that when these precious bids came to us, we were no longer outsiders. We had the inside track to win these projects because the RFPs appeared to have been written based on the proprietary information they were gleaning directly from the blog posts I had been putting into the information eco-system.

In less than 18 months from the moment we started our social media strategy, we were awarded $47 million in new business, all of it directed to the 10 target solutions we had strategized from the beginning.

While Sander has a remarkable and inspiring story, it is by no means unique. Businesses of all sizes from start-ups to global enterprises, service companies to commodity producers, and health care providers to defense giants, are using these ideas to create measurable business benefits.

Let's dissect Sander's case study to see how it applies to the five foundational strategies covered in this book.

Humans buy from humans

I think one of the most powerful lines in Sanders' testimony was, "We did the work."

All too often our companies want to outsource human connection to an agency, administrative assistant, or marketing department. Sander realized that to re-build these terribly damaged relationships he would have to depend on a radical amount of goodwill and trust. He needed to show up. He needed to do the work.

As an experienced sales professional, he knew he couldn't

delegate trust and his social media presence was treated as an extension of his human presence.

The other notable aspect of his connection was patience. The leadership team allowed him the time necessary to do the job right. This was not a month-long campaign or managed against a quarterly sales objective. Relationships take time and he committed to building his new connections in a way that would be meaningful, perhaps even loyalty ...

Small interactions lead to loyalty

I thought this part of Sander's plan was particularly well-executed.

Did you notice that he went to wherever the customer was getting their information? He resisted the ego-driven goal of driving people to his company's website and social properties. He took the more human and humble approach of seeking to connect with customers where they naturally were hanging out and gathering information. Company LinkedIn Groups. Industry forums. Twitter.

By providing a drip, drip, drip of small, consistent and helpful provocations – even if it meant giving a nod to the competition -- he established himself as a trusted source of valuable content. Eventually, his new connections liked him enough and trusted him enough to send him an opportunity to bid on projects. Boom. The birthday party!

And he's not stopping now. Just as human friendships need to be tended and nurtured, so do our online business relationships. It's not a campaign. It's a person.

The social media mindset

I'm generally a conservative business professional who won't "guarantee" much in this world. But I will guarantee this. Sander never would have gotten back into the good graces of his estranged customer through the traditional cold calls and old selling techniques. At least not in this decade!

Sander moved his world view from "selling" to "teaching, helping, and serving" and this powerfully distinguished him from his competition.

Meaningful content that was targeted, original, and written with individual decision-makers in mind became the centerpiece of his initiative.

He systematically, mindfully, and even scientifically researched his potential audience and connected to them on their terms and in their space.

His over-arching mission was to be authentically helpful. Frankly, that can be a pretty unnerving position for an organization. But I think the sheer desperation of the situation – absolutely no sales from this customer – forced the company culture to embrace something, anything, that could change the game.

The information eco-system

In this piece, Sander focused on the blogs, LinkedIn, and Twitter posts that enabled his strategy. But in fact, there was also a team effort going on behind the scenes to help support his initiative. The company support team provided the training and professional editing he needed to succeed, measurement and monitoring tools to capture progress, as well as a state-of-the-art, beautiful, and functional showcase for his content -- the company blog.

The central marketing team also produced podcasts, videos, white papers, slide presentations, infographics, and eBooks to supplement Sander's personal output and surround the customers with answers to any kind of question, on any topic, in any online venue where the customer happened to be. Through this diligent and comprehensive program of content creation in relevant platforms, they gave their products the best chance to be discovered.

Content as catalyst

I'm probably most proud of the way Sander was able to execute on the content development training I provided. This allowed him to approach his content strategy with wisdom and confidence. He was laser-focused on providing content that was excellent, timely, interesting, relevant and perhaps even a little entertaining. He brought his personality into the content which helped build connection and trust.

He was also mindful that the content would not work unless it was IGNITED. Every social media strategy needs a content plan and a network plan and Sander worked hard to find and connect with an audience who was receptive to his content. He didn't just "blog" to check a box. He created content that was discovered, shared, and discussed. And that made all the difference.

In fact, a $47 million difference.

In the final section of this book, I'll provide a short overview of some of the major social media platforms, but this concludes the actual "content" portion of the book.

I know you have a lot going against you. Time. Emergencies. Budget cuts. Cultural obstinacy. Stubborn bosses. Aggressive competitors.

There is no book in the world that can make these problems go away. But I do hope that *Social Media Explained* has given you the confidence, inspiration, and pearls of wisdom to know that social media marketing is powerful, and it works.

It worked for Sander and thousands of my customers, students, and blog readers are figuring this out too. Slowly, steadily they are creating an effective human social media presence fueled by truly helpful content and a consistent and authentic level of engagement.

You.

Can.

Do.

This.

Thank you for reading my book. Stay in touch, won't you?

A Social Media Platform Primer

I hope you've enjoyed *Social Media Explained* and feel more confident about entering the world of social media.

It might seem weird to go through a social media book without concrete lessons on Facebook, Twitter, and their digital brethren but this was by design. If I took that approach, your head would have been spinning, you would have become disheartened … and probably stopped reading by now. And then there is the fact that whatever I wrote would have been out of date by the time you reached this point any way!

I'm confident that if you have reached this point in the book you know enough about social media marketing to determine an appropriate strategy for your company.

Still, it might be useful to at least cover some of the major platforms on a high level and there are a few things I would like to convey about the platforms … maybe bust a few myths and share a few secrets with you. So here are a few essential truths you should keep in mind on some of the "majors."

Blogs

Blogs are among the most important sources of "rich" content – the real fuel for your social media engine.

The oldest form of social media, blogs give the average web user the ability to publish long-form content quickly and easily. Instead of static websites, blogs are interactive in nature, allowing visitors to leave a comment on individual articles or blog posts. Many newspaper websites and even online magazines now operate like blogs as readers have the ability to post comments on articles.

Blogs began as online diaries, giving people the ability to share their thoughts and ideas online. However, in time, blogs grew in popularity to become a common and powerful tool used by businesses. In fact, many company websites are built on blogging platforms to allow website owners to easily upload content.

Today, blogs can support many different business strategies – attracting employees, helping out customer service, even supporting R&D. Some companies have hundreds of blogs segmented by verticals, regions, product lines and customer demographics.

One key idea about blogging: It can be a powerful source of search engine traffic. Some companies have a blog separate from their website. That never makes sense. Why not drive people to your website? That's where business gets done. Don't let anybody talk you into a separate blog. It should be integrated into your website.

To learn more about starting and nurturing a blog, you might enjoy my book *Born to Blog* (McGraw Hill 2013).

Podcasting

Podcasting is sort of like audio blogging, and another potential source of rich content.

Although a mature technology, the platform has been experiencing a renaissance because of the growing use of mobile devices. It's become easy to carry these "radio programs" anywhere you go and listen while multi-tasking, driving or working out.

While the popularity of podcasting has created a whole new generation of radio "celebrities," adoption of this platform in a corporate setting has lagged behind almost any other social channel.

Starting and maintaining a podcast is the most technically complicated channel and may require a modest investment in audio technology ... and some practice!

My insider tip on podcasting: Because of the slow adoption by many companies, look at podcasting carefully as a potential niche point of differentiation for your business.

If you want to learn more about podcasting, I recommend a visit to Dr. Jon Buscall and his website www.jontusmedia.com. He has a lot of great resources available on podcasting as well as an extremely helpful eBook on the subject.

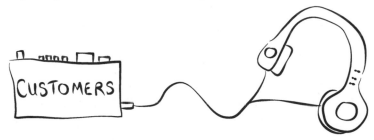

Twitter is the darling of everybody from marketers and celebrities to teens and members of the media thanks to its in-the-moment and public nature.

Unless you choose to keep your messages private, everything you post on Twitter is available for the world to see. In today's social media-driven world, breaking news often comes in the form of a tweet.

Twitter has also become the de facto "second screen" for commentary while viewing television and has attracted a lot of attention for the advertising "ripple" it is causing with its new relationship with TV.

This platform has many advantages for businesses. It's probably the fastest way to grow a targeted audience and Twitter has also introduced a variety of advertising platforms. Most brands are now utilizing Twitter as an extension of the customer service department. Research shows that people who follow your brand on Twitter tend to be very loyal.

There are probably as many ways to use Twitter as there are business strategies. But my view is the most powerful advantage is networking. The open and public nature of Twitter allows you to develop relationships with new customers, potential employees, and business partners in your region and beyond. If your business can benefit from live networking events, it can benefit from Twitter.

My inside Twitter tip is to explore the advanced search function on Twitter. Many marketers believe this is one of the most powerful sources for marketing research and insight ever created … and it's free! You can save Twitter searches to monitor discussions about brands, watch competitors, and discover new customer wants and needs.

The biggest downside to Twitter is that it is difficult to understand, which inhibits adoption.

It's like entering a new world with a different language and a new set of customs. To de-mystify Twitter, many people have benefitted from *The Tao of Twitter* (McGraw-Hill 2014), the best-selling book on Twitter in the world.

What began as a network for college students has transformed into the biggest social network and the largest website in the world today. In my classes I teach that Facebook isn't a website, it's a lifestyle for many people. It is global, addictive, useful and the largest media entity in history. You can't ignore it.

Despite its popularity, no platform has created more controversy or angst. It was so cavalier with the private information of its users that it was indicted by the U.S. government, investigated by a Congressional Committee and found guilty. It has been the source of tragic teen bullying and abuse. The company's botched IPO disappointed investors and tarnished its reputation. The company has been repeatedly criticized for being unfriendly and unresponsive to its business customers.

And yet ...

Facebook is unsurpassed in its ability to connect businesses with its customers in a rapid and human way. It is an ideal platform to spread the word quickly, monitor reactions, and collect data.

Facebook has been improving its analytics capabilities and ad reporting systems. Since becoming a public company it has been focusing on new revenue streams and advertising platforms, particularly on mobile.

Many business owners look at Facebook and are lulled into thinking that this is a "free" way to sell your stuff. In reality, achieving success on Facebook may be one of the most difficult and expensive propositions out there. Here's why ...

Facebook uses a formula known as Edge Rank to edit everyone's "timeline," which is the daily news feed that appears from a user's list of friends. Because of this editing process, your message is normally seen by less than one-fifth of the people who follow you.

To increase the odds that your message will be seen, you can either pay Facebook money to make it a "sponsored post," buy ads, or devote resources to create outstanding content that has a chance to breakthrough Edge Rank ... and you probably need to do a combination of all of these. Even if you're doing an outstanding job with your content every day, you may still be nearly invisible.

So my insider tip on Facebook is to approach this platform rationally and realize that marketing effectively on this channel is neither easy nor cheap!

LinkedIn

LinkedIn is considered the social network for professionals. LinkedIn showcases your business experience and connects you with contacts from your email address book and places you've worked.

LinkedIn Profiles are much like an online resume, detailing your education, skills, experience and recommendations from your colleagues and friends. It also gives you the opportunity to link to presentations, blog posts and your portfolio. The platform has transformed the HR profession. Among the major social platforms, it is unsurpassed as a place for sales leads and connections, particularly if you are in B2B.

There are nearly 2 million LinkedIn Groups devoted to every professional vocation, company, and cause imaginable. Some of them are noisy and spammy, but many are populated with caring professionals who devote a lot of time and caring while helping people in their groups.

The downside of LinkedIn can be summed up by this tweet I received the other day: "I must be really bored. I checked in to LinkedIn to see what was going on."

Despite the fact that LinkedIn has continually innovated and is a multimedia powerhouse of a platform, the truth is, it is normally a little boring there. There just isn't much socialization going on.

For my insider tip, I'd like to help you make a link between blogging, LinkedIn and building a relevant and engaged social media audience.

If you are ever stuck for an idea for your content plan, go to your favorite LinkedIn Group for your industry. Each group has a place where members can post questions and ideas relevant to the topic of the group. Find an interesting question and write a blog post as an answer. Then, go back to the group and post a link to your post as an answer to the question, in an authentically helpful way.

This simple exercise has accomplished three important objectives at one time. First, it has provided a source of meaningful content for your blog. Second, it has provided a kind and helpful service to the person who asked the question. You will certainly be on their radar screen now. And third, by answering the question with a link, you are driving highly relevant eyeballs to your web site. This system is efficient and it really works.

Pinterest

If you are in a business related to fashion, style, food, travel, interior design, or crafts, Pinterest is a must. The addictive site can be described as scrapbooks of ideas, dreams, inspirations, and aspirational purchases.

The user base is more than 70 percent women and it is now one of the top five social media platforms in terms of active users. Pinterest is practically made for business. Where "selling" is discouraged on other sites, Pinterest fans actively look for images of favorite products, with the price tag included, and many of these users are ready to buy. In fact "pins" with price tags garner 36 percent more likes than those that don't. The average American Pinterest user spends 1 hour and 17 minutes on the website per visit.

Here is the most important thing to know about Pinterest. It drives more web traffic and actual purchases than any other platform, including Facebook. The Social Habit Report from Edison Research showed that Pinterest users not only click on photos to find the original source, they also go to company sites after leaving Pinterest, inspired by the photos they have seen there.

If you want people to start pinning from your website (which is an incredibly efficient way of spreading the word about your business) then you have to make your website and blog very visual. Spend some time on Pinterest getting to know the style, subject and compositions of the photos your potential customers are "pinning."

Google +

While we may value choice in real life, on the Internet, we usually only have the bandwidth to dedicate to one platform. We like to have a choice among car brands or breakfast cereals, but we only need one Twitter. We only want one LinkedIn. And we only need one social network ... which would be Facebook.

There lies the problem for Google Plus. After several failed attempts to launch social networks, Google placed a high bet on a late entry to take on Facebook. Although the number of registered users places it among the top five platforms, adoption has been relatively slow because it is trying to unseat Facebook as the preferred social network, and that is a pretty difficult task.

Failing to achieve organic growth, the company is increasingly tying activity on Google Plus to search engine placement, integration with all of the Google utilities, and other Google-related benefits, virtually forcing businesses to participate.

Don't get me wrong. G+ is a terrific site with many wonderful features (most notably the popular Hangouts utility). It has a host of loyal fans, but it is virtually ignored by the core 15-34 year-old social media audience, and is invisible in the traditional media, where Facebook, Twitter, and YouTube dominate.

Research by the University of Massachusetts showed that about one-third of the Fortune 500 companies are on Google Plus compared to about 90 percent for Facebook, and among those G+ accounts, more than half are inactive. This statistic represents both the problem and opportunity.

For those new to the platform it may seem a bit of a ghost town. But if you are late to the social media scene and want to carve a niche, G+ may be your entry ticket. Although many customers may not frequent the site, if you learn to master the platform, you may connect with Google loyalists and reap unique search engine benefits.

Just a few years ago, the most popular videos on YouTube were home-made productions of squirrels on water skis and brides falling into swimming pools. Those days are over.

Today, YouTube is mainstream entertainment, viewed by commuters on bullet trains and at home on big screen TVs. We are in a video-crazy world and experts predict the percent of video-related content we will consume in the next few years could double.

Brands are capitalizing by creating increasingly-epic mini-movies exclusively for their dedicated YouTube channels. The bar for quality is constantly going up.

In addition to feeding the public's nearly insatiable hunger for video content, companies also realize that YouTube is owned by Google and is the second-largest search engine in the world. Billions of videos are watched on YouTube every day.

It may seem daunting trying to enter this crowded world of Hollywood-quality videos but there is still room for even small businesses in this space. Remember that search results are typically local so even start-ups have a chance to compete for attention with useful, informative and entertaining videos.

My insider tip for YouTube is to concentrate on creating practical, informative how-to videos. While it might be every entrepreneur's dream to create a "viral" video, the fact is, "Gangnam Style" is not something you can really plan for.

However, many businesses are ruling the air waves (and search results) with simple, even crude, videos to help solve problems.

I was recently at an outdoor supply store looking to buy some fishing gear. I wanted to learn how to fish for bass. I was lucky to run into a local (who looked to be about 80 years old) who offered to help me pick out the right kind of rod and tackle. He started showing me how to put the hook on a specialized lure and then paused and said, "You know, you need to look this up on YouTube. You can learn how to do anything there."

That's what I mean!

SlideShare

SlideShare is not normally considered a "major" social media platform but I wanted to include it in this overview because as you consider populating your information eco-system, this might be an excellent place to start.

The idea is simple: Share PowerPoint slides. And every company has PowerPoint slides, right?

When I first started teaching college courses a few years ago I learned first-hand how powerful SlideShare can be. Before my first class, I uploaded my presentation slides on to SlideShare so my students could see my teaching materials without printing them out.

One hour after they had been uploaded, the slides had already been viewed 150 times! None of those viewers were my students – they had not even met me yet. I realized that SlideShare could also be a business development opportunity so I added a final slide to the deck – for more information on this topic, please visit my website and www.businessesGROW.com. The platform has become an important traffic source for my business.

SlideShare is highly indexed by Google and, because you can add relevant keywords when you upload your slides, you can help people find your content efficiently. A few business professionals I know use SlideShare extensively for business development because it is so easy and normally overlooked by most businesses!

Photo sites

Instagram and Flickr are the dominant photo-sharing sites but I wanted to group the category together because I expect this to be an explosive area for social media in the next few years.

The importance of photo-oriented content is being driven by a couple of market factors.

First, the use of mobile smart devices has brought the barriers to creating and sharing photographic content down to zero. It's fun, it's easy, it's fast.

Second, in our information-dense world, we may only have time to consume photos. It's easy to fill a few seconds of spare time thumbing through Instagram photos.

Finally, you can do it at work. Many companies may block access to Facebook or Twitter on company computers, but people can easily sneak some time with a site like Instagram on their smartphone. The Social Habit research showed that 85 percent of the people who use Instagram do it at work, easily the most work-friendly social media site around.

If you are a "visual" brand, the emerging popularity of photo sites can be a goldmine of opportunity. An insider tip – don't look at photo sites only as a place for sharing. This can be an incredibly useful place to do market discovery work and customer research by searching through topics and hashtags. How can you find, involve, and reward customers for sharing their brand experiences over photo sites?

This concludes the third and final section of *Social Media Explained*. Thanks so much for reading my book. Good luck with your social media journey!

Mark W. Schaefer

About the Author

Mark W. Schaefer is a globally-recognized blogger, speaker, educator, business consultant, and author who blogs at {grow} — one of the top marketing blogs of the world. Mark has worked in global sales, PR, and marketing positions for nearly 30 years and now provides consulting services as Executive Director of U.S.-based Schaefer Marketing Solutions. He specializes in social media training and clients include both start-ups and global brands such as IBM, Johnson & Johnson, and the UK government.

Mark has advanced degrees in marketing and organizational development and is a faculty member of the graduate studies program at Rutgers University.

He is the author of three other best-selling books, *Return On Influence*, *Born to Blog*, and *The Tao of Twitter*, the best-selling book on Twitter in the world. He is among the world's most recognized social media authorities and has been a keynote speaker at many conferences around the world including Social Media Week London, National Economic Development Association, the Institute for International and European Affairs (an EU think tank) and Word of Mouth Marketing Summit Tokyo.

You can stay connected with Mark at www.businessesGROW.com

About the Illustrator

Joey Strawn is a marketing director, cartoonist, husband, entrepreneur, and general purveyor of awesomeness. He is currently the Integrated Marketing Director at Industrial Strength Marketing in Nashville, TN, working with industrial and B2B businesses to increase revenue using digital marketing strategies.

Joey has been in the digital strategy business for nearly a decade and has worked on digital marketing campaigns for national casual dining chains, Fortune 500 industrial manufacturers and everything in between.

Joey has a Masters in Marketing Communications from Boston University and has been mixing business strategy with cartoons for almost 3 years through his own blog and on www.businesses-GROW.com via the {growtoons}. He is an adjunct professor at Lipscomb University teaching Social Media Strategy in the English and Communications departments.

Stay connected to Joey on Twitter at @joey_strawn.

Acknowledgments

When I married my wife Rebecca I was a businessman who was a part-time writer.

Today, I am primarily a writer who is a part-time businessman.

There is a BIG difference!

I am able to create content through blog posts, videos, and books like *Social Media Explained* only because I have a spouse who tolerates and supports the strange and often inconvenient world of the creative process. Thank you honey!

The creative team of Joey and Amanda Strawn made this project a joy and inserted an entirely new level of fun into the arduous process of creating a major manuscript. Creating a Vonnegut-like book filled with doodles is a dream come true!

Annette A. Penney has been the woman behind the scenes on a number of my books now through her tireless and exceptional input and editing. Nothing lights my day more than when the brilliant Annette adds a comment like "This is awesome!" to my manuscript!

If you are a reader of my blog {grow} you have unwittingly been a focus group for the ideas in this book! Much of the content began its life as a blog post. I carefully watched the comment section for ideas, corrections, additions, and dissent. This book was forged by an incredibly intelligent and loyal social media audience. Thank you one and all!

Finally, every word I write, every breath I take, comes through the grace of God. I humbly submit this work to His Glory.

Index

A

Amazon   66
American Coalition of Clean Coal 67
AT&T   28
Audi   58
Azhar, Azeem   44-45

B

Bank of Ireland 30
Baer Jay   112
Benny, Jack   22
Berle, Milton   22
Bicycle Brand Playing Cards   68
Biehn, Sander   115
Blend-Tec   108
Blogging   19, 23-25, 28, 42-43, 48, 56-58
    Basics 124
    Benefits   56-58
    as Rich content 43, 110-111, 124
    Strategy   100-102,111, 128
Born to Blog   28, 125
Boston University   135
Buscall, Jon   125
Business Networking International 86

C

Caterpillar   58
CBS Morning News   41
Celtic manor Resort   30
Cemex 76
Citi   58
Coca-Cola   106
Content Marketing   25-29, 35-40, 41-48, 117-121

D

Depend Adult Diapers   66-67
Dessert Gallery 13
Disney 16, 108
Dowling, Tony   23-27, 29-30
Dutch Government   75

E

eBay   66
Edison Research   11, 18, 77, 99, 129, 132
Essilor International   75-76
Etsy   66

F

Facebook   4-5, 10-13, 19, 25-27, 34, 42, 68-69, 72, 79, 98-99, 101-102, 111, 124, 130, 132
    Edge Rank   127
    Groups   80
    and Schools   96
    Search tool   36, 67, 77
    Statistics   13, 26, 38, 77, 80, 99
    Strategy   79, 109, 126-127
Falling Skies   43
Farmville   108
Ferrell, Will   78
Flickr 132
Fonderia Pontificia Marinelli   69

G

Gangnam Style 27
Gladwell, Malcolm   26
Google   34, 42, 76-77, 131
Google+   129-130
Grow blog   27